Don't

Sit

the

Bench

Building Self-Esteem and
Confidence for Success

LOUIS S. SAPIA, JR.

MINDSTIR MEDIA

Published by Mindstir Media, LLC
45 Lafayette Rd | Suite 181| North Hampton, NH 03862 | USA
1.800.767.0531 | www.mindstirmedia.com

Printed in the United States of America
ISBN-13: 978-1-958729-38-0

Contents

Forewords

In this thoughtful, down-to-earth, very readable book, Louis (Lou) Sapia, Jr. does what any good coach does. He explains game strategies, draws up the plays, and coaches each player to develop and use skills, motivation, and determination to play their best game. Lou Sapia, Jr. provides great mentoring advice as well as life-coping strategies for various educational, work, and life settings for people of all ages and skill levels.

Lou and I worked together for many years as colleagues at the same college. I saw him practice the practical guidance he outlines in *Don't Sit the Bench* as he worked with students of all backgrounds, abilities, and ages. He mentored, taught, cared about, and helped each person to become more than they thought they could be. After graduation, Lou helped students find and grow in their careers. The ideas, advice, and mentoring Lou offers in this book are well tested in the real world. In this book, Lou encourages readers to have an understanding of head and heart, intellect, courage, and the drive to keep finding ways to succeed. He offers easy to follow ideas and strategies to turn knowledge and goals into achievable life-changing actions.

Lou explains how early life experiences create ways of thinking and feeling that influence our self-esteem. He challenges the reader to push beyond those limiting self-assessments and to find ways to make adjustments, to be flexible, find our own voices, and to get in the game. Lou outlines how resilience, personal responsibility, persistence, observing and learning from other successful role models, and trying a variety of options to find our own way forward can all lead to happiness and a fuller life.

Don't Sit the Bench explains how a sense of belonging, finding ways to build and maintain connections, understanding the importance of changing course if you are not gifted at one thing, and finding ways to leverage small goals into larger ones are necessary for growth. This book is full of what feels like personalized coaching and offers encouragement to every reader. The book walks you through a series of ways to get in the game. It's up to you to put in the work. Ultimately, that is the message of *Don't Sit the Bench*. If you don't like the way your life is going, get some coaching on how to change it, and then put in the work. Lou's book is full of great coaching advice.

—Dr. Jean Egan, Ph.D., CFLE, Professor, Social and Behavioral Sciences

I had the privilege of taking a class from Louis (Lou) Sapia during my time at college. Towards the end of my time in his class, he encouraged and assisted me in preparing my resume and finding a job without any hesitation.

Lou is a great professor and software architect. This book is filled with his real-life experiences of how to become goal oriented, prioritize your tasks, and manage your time and finances. You'll also learn how to create a professional network and seek better opportunities. It teaches how to avoid negative energy and be grateful for what you have. I am so impressed with his book! It has great empathy for young people and is a great motivator to pursue your dreams.

I highly recommend this book to the youth and anyone who wants to empower themselves, avoid stress, and be grateful to achieve success.

—Harish Bhatt, Senior Business Intelligence Developer

In the following chapters Louis (Lou) Sapia has set forth a foundation of career and life concepts and illustrated many of these with his real-life experiences. I witnessed his struggle from very humble beginnings and saw in real time his success and failures that make him who he is today.

Without question I believe Lou is the personification of the famous quote by Thomas Jefferson: "I'm a great believer in luck, and I find the harder I work the more I have of it." Being a person of great empathy for young people who are trying to become independent and others who are struggling, he is capturing the hard-fought gems of practical knowledge and wisdom that can make such a great difference for people.

Having walked the walk with him through the years, as I read the chapters I pondered how these comprehensive concepts (little discussed in the educational system) would have made my life easier and far less stressful. I would recommend this book to those struggling and to those mentors (parents or others) who can present these concepts to the ones they care about. This is all presented in an intriguing manner that makes the reader eager to read the next chapter.

I recommend this with the sentiment of wishing the reader to be empowered such that they spend less time in stress and turmoil and more time living!

Enjoy the read.

**—Chris Bevans, Manager and
Solution Architect, Information Technology**

We are young, eager, and setting out to make a difference in the world. We have dreams and goals and a tremendous amount of excitement about all of what the future holds. Those two sentences often define what a kid coming out of high school or even in the first year at college might be feeling. Then the reality of college hits them, and their life is drastically different and much more challenging. Suddenly, the time and energy that a young person must negotiate is challenged at every turn. No longer is your mother or father taking care of the little things like laundry, food, getting you up in the morning, and helping you make time for study. What happens when what you are doing (college/ higher education) is now all up to you, and how do you make productive use of your time and energy?

Colleges make money, so they have thousands of students; keeping those tuitions coming is imperative, and there is no thought about the effect that some of their systems may have on a student. Often a young person is required to take a test at 10 pm (because you're given an exam time through a lottery) after taking two other exams that same day. This young adult gets to his/her/their university at 8 am and leaves at 11 pm. This incredible time crunch requires them to skip meals or shove anything (likely fast food and nutritionally depleted) in their mouth with a lot of caffeine just to keep going. This is an extreme case, but one I know firsthand from my best friend's son, who is a hard-working student and doing well in college yet still exhausted. It is essential to understand time management at this point, prioritize actions and find strategies to make these new responsibilities doable.

That is precisely what Louis Sapia has done in his book **Don't Sit The Bench.** He gives a student guidelines on how one is meant to negotiate this new way of existing, sometimes from simply surviving to a way to thrive. **Don't Sit the Bench** gives the reader practical ways to manage time and ways to view this new world and encourages a young person to find that mentor that will carry a torch for them (even if just in their mind's eye) to keep them able to stay the course. There is a huge advantage to becoming good at *living* life so that the learning one is receiving is taken into your brain without disruption.

The other thing Louis does so beautifully here is that he shares his life experiences as proof that what he is sharing works. He also gives you ways to view entrepreneurship that make logical and practical sense. Everything that this book addresses is so needed and so ignored. Few are taught or explained what the real world will be like and what to do when you get there. Louis Sapia has written a mandatory book for anyone with dreams who wants to see those dreams become realities. You just have to put in the work; then, there is no reason not to succeed if the right game plan is set in motion.

—Mariel Hemingway

"As a society we need to balance protecting children from the world and teaching skills to face it."

—*Louis S. Sapia, Jr.*

Chapter 1

Find Your
Game

*"If you can't fly then run, if you can't run then
walk, if you can't walk then crawl, but whatever
you do you have to keep moving forward."*

—MARTIN LUTHER KING, JR.

The title of this book, while a metaphor, has a degree of reality to it in my life. It is something I experienced and, years later, looked back and realized there was a lesson to pass on.

❧ Sitting The Bench

During my middle school years, I played basketball in the Christian Youth Organization (CYO) league. I wasn't very good, so I sat on the bench at every game and rarely got to play. If I did play, it was only because my team had a big lead, and the closing minutes of the game meant there was no way I could affect the outcome. Even at practice, the coach focused on the good players while I sat and watched.

I remember, vividly, sitting on the bench watching other teammates play and hoping that our team would generate a big enough lead so that I might be able to get in the game. There were substitutions to provide rest for the starting players but, even then, I wasn't called on to play as there were substitutes better than me.

The cheerleaders were impressed with the starting players as well as others who played often and mingled with them after the game, at school and at social events. I wasn't disliked but, certainly, no one went out of their way to speak to me. This period in my life was humiliating because not only was I not playing in the games and gaining skills, but I also wasn't participating socially either. I wanted to, but the good players had the advantage of being popular because of their playing so they fit in socially more than I could.

While I was struggling for acceptance with my peers, nothing was more humiliating to me than the warmup shooting sessions before the start of each game. The other benchwarmers and I were not allowed to shoot the ball. Our job was to rebound the ball and pass it on to the starting five players so that they could practice their shots. With cheerleaders watching, I was embarrassed. I wish I could have thought of something to avoid that part of the game, but I could think of nothing. I was totally humiliated.

Joining a team where I didn't play impeded any chance to improve at team basketball. Afterall, how could I improve if I wasn't playing with the team in the games or at practice? Certainly, I could go out on my own and practice at the park, and I did do that. But it's not the same as mixing in with a team and finding harmony among your teammates. By playing with your teammates, you get to know how each one performs and what to expect of them so that the team is cohesive and in sync. If I never get to play with the team, how could I be expected to perform at the same capacity as the others? Joining a band is the same thing. If you only practice alone and never with the band, it would be difficult to find harmony.

Thus far I've been talking about my inability to improve my basketball skills and my unpopularity. While that was unfortunate, I learned years later there was something much worse—the stagnation of my self-esteem. I lost confidence as a basketball player and my self-esteem was shattered. I was afraid to join other sports and refrained from mingling with my peers. When I met new people, both younger and older, I didn't speak.

Those who played the game, of course, benefitted by improving their basketball skills, but more importantly the development of their social skills. Because of their success on the basketball court both boys and girls wanted to socialize with them. The players loved to talk about their playing experiences amongst teammates as well as team members from other teams and the cheerleaders gravitated to them. While they didn't realize it, they were developing their self-worth and social skills. As for me, I felt like someone outside looking in. It was a very discouraging feeling at the time, and I didn't know how to fix it.

I'm not sharing this story as a victim, but rather to help you understand the value of what I learned. I realized years later the importance self-esteem to reach success in life. It is the very foundation that young people need to develop by doing things that help them feel good about themselves. While some people may feel just fine sitting on the bench, it didn't suit me so I should have found something I was good at instead. Certainly, I wanted to be a part of the basketball social group, but if it wasn't working and it was resulting in stunting my personal growth, I should have searched for something that contributed positively to my self-esteem rather than negatively. For example, I'd been a long-distance runner for many years and had great endurance so I should have joined the track team. Another sport that requires endurance and running is soccer, so I should have tried that sport. Or maybe taking up an instrument.

Finding My Game

I was always a studious individual, so I did feel good about my grades. While that wasn't helping my popularity among my peers, it helped me find self-worth. I realized that through hard work I could achieve good grades and that felt empowering. I gained a great deal of respect from my teachers, so it felt good to receive some appreciation in that sense. This experience taught me that when I work hard to achieve good grades, I have something I can control. It wasn't dependent on performing with a team, just me. I also felt the hard work and good grades would manifest into something greater in my life.

High school can be a challenging time for some, and it certainly was for me. I was suffering with an identity crisis. It was easier for those who excelled at sports to fit in, but I wasn't one of them. I often felt lost and not quite sure what group of kids I should hang out with. I felt I needed to belong to some social group, so I ended up hanging out with kids in the same social economic class as me, where education wasn't all that important and money was scarce. We hung out in the streets and partied. We never talked about our future after high school. Instead, we seemed to complain about what we didn't have, acting much like victims. Some friends turned to drugs and ended up in tragic life situations, even death.

While I hung out with these group of kids regularly, there was one day each school term when I felt I couldn't socialize with them… report card day. That was the day I avoided them because they got together to complain about their bad grades, and I had nothing to complain about. My grades were good, and I made honor roll. I found the one thing in my life that improved my self-worth and that was my academic successes. But even with good grades, I didn't pursue college out of high school. College wasn't important in my family, work was, so my brother and sisters were pushed to find work rather than pursue higher education after high school.

I found a full-time job at a paint store that didn't pay much and had no future. Some of my friends went to college the first fall semester after high school and I'm not sure why I didn't do the same. It seems like I was back sitting on the bench watching others achieve success. Even today I don't quite know why my mind wasn't focused on college. Sure, my parents never talked about college for me, they wanted me to work, but I've had to figure things out for myself since I was very young so why I didn't consider college at that time I don't know. I do know I felt lost and unsure of what would become of me, and I didn't know what to do. This example demonstrates the importance of mentorship which I address later in Chapter 10.

After a year of working at the paint store I realized I was not achieving anything. I didn't learn any worthwhile skills and my self-esteem was still suffering. I decided it was time to quit and attend college full time to study computer science at a community college. Right after I applied, I felt a positive change in my self-worth.

At college I embraced my courses and, like high school, studied hard. Studying was the sole activity that made me feel good in high school and now it had the same effect on me in college. But another positive effect from attending college was my improved social life. I found friends like me, who did not have the funds to attend the more expensive universities but wanted an education none the less. Like me, they wanted good grades and to make something of themselves and we shared the same goals. I became popular very quickly now that I found my niche. I was no longer a spectator watching others succeed, I was now a participant.

This book is about finding the right path to developing confidence and self-esteem as well as making the right decisions towards personal and professional growth. The first step on that path is to find something that makes you feel good about yourself. "Find your game," so-to-speak. If sitting on the bench being a part of a team makes you feel good and adds to your self-esteem, there is nothing wrong with that. But if you are like me and need to feel like a participant, find something that does it for you. A sport, music, drama, or simply learning and getting good grades as I did. It may not be popular but that doesn't matter if you feel good about it. For example, I used to take ballroom dancing lessons. My friends thought it was strange and made fun of me. But I didn't care, I liked it and felt good about it. I got to meet many new friends and we enjoyed ourselves going out after classes dancing.

Your personal development is dependent on feeling good by building your self-esteem so that you can get the most out of life. Try new things until you find a fit. If you fail, you still win because you will have learned what you don't like as well as what your weaknesses and strengths are. Being aware of your strengths and weaknesses will better prepare you for successes and challenges throughout your life as life is full of ups and downs. By trying until you succeed you will learn more about your identity. Also, it will help you understand your capacity so that you can decide the right paths forward.

When I turned twenty, I started long-distance running and weightlifting. I found running was very natural for me and ran about eighteen miles a week. I also entered several 5k, 10k, and 20k races. Days I didn't run I lifted weights and enjoyed feeling healthy and confident. Running and weightlifting has had a significant impact on my mental and physical well-being and my confidence must have shown because people were now gravitating to me. I continue with my exercise regimen still today, forty years later. There is a connection between physical and mental health, and feeling healthy naturally helps you possess a positive outlook in life.

🌸 Unplanned Opportunities

I have learned that taking on new interests and opportunities often results in other opportunities I never thought of. For example, years ago I planned and managed my wedding using my computer programming skills. The restaurant where my reception took place needed reports on my guests such as food choices, seat arrangements at each table, and the names of each guest. When I handed my reports in for the wedding reception the employees at the restaurant were shocked and impressed with my reports. They liked the way I had done it so much they were going to use my reports as templates for others to follow. It wasn't my intention to impress, only to fulfil the task of delivering the required information for the reception. But now, this gave me an idea.

Because I planned and managed my wedding using my computer skills and the restaurant employees were impressed, I came up with the idea of developing a software product called the "Simple Wedding Planner." This product allowed everyone else to plan their wedding accordingly. So, taking on the challenge of planning my wedding led me to a new opportunity I didn't plan.

I spent six months developing the wedding planner product. This was before the days of the internet, so I planned on creating CD versions of the software product. I had to come up with money for marketing and production, so I decided to find a part-time job to fund it rather than use the money my wife and I planned for the household. I was taking a financial risk funding the project, so it was better to use money that wasn't planned as a married couple.

I saw an opportunity to become a part-time limousine driver and I was about to pursue that when I saw an ad in the newspaper to teach computer programming at a non-credit technical school. I applied and got the job.

I had never taught before, so I was very nervous the first couple of days. But after a week of teaching, I realized I found it very natural, and I enjoyed it. Soon teaching became my passion. I enjoyed being creative by coming up with different techniques, strategies, and assignments resulting in students succeeding in the classroom. Now that I found my true passion, the wedding planner product was no longer on my mind. Instead, finding better teaching opportunities became my new goal.

After teaching at the technical school for six months, I decided I wanted to teach at credited colleges and universities. But to do so I needed my master's degree. I was age forty-two at the time and I never thought about returning to school for a master's degree. But now I was driven to do so to further my teaching career.

I was determined to get my teaching career at the college level on track as soon as possible. So, I crammed the courses required for my master's degree and was able to finish it within a year while working full-time. I did basically nothing for a year but study and work.

A couple of months before graduation I started looking for adjunct courses to teach and was hired right after graduation at two different institutions, University of Connecticut and Manchester Community College. Five years later I became a full-time professor and authored my first book three years after that on database design and programming.

Imagine, all that activity started with the planning of my wedding and manifested into becoming a college professor and author. That's what I mean by continuing to look for interests and challenges to help you seek opportunities you never thought of and develop into someone you had no idea you would be.

Finding your interests doesn't just apply to work and school-related activities. They can be fun too. In 2012 I was searching on the internet to learn if one of my favorite bands, The J. Geils Band, was on tour. While searching I found that the band was scheduled to be in an Adam Sandler movie called *Grown Ups 2* and filming was taking place in Swampscott, Massachusetts, which is two and a half hours from where I lived in Connecticut. I found the band being in the movie interesting and wondered how that came about so I looked further into it. I quickly learned that the movie production company was looking for doubles to play the band members. I applied and to my great surprise I got a call two days later offering me the job to double for the bass player. It was an exciting experience meeting several celebrities and pretending to play bass on a stage in front of about three hundred extras.

But I also took interest in how the production crews were making the movie. I found it to be a wonderful learning experience and it left me appreciative of movie making. So much so that if I were starting my career over, I might have pursued a career in the movie industry making movies as opposed to acting in them. Imagine, I never thought I would be in a movie and learn about movie making but my interest in a band brought that to life.

Create Challenges

We don't have to wait for challenges to come to us. We can create our own challenges. When I was younger, I feared public speaking, so I did everything to avoid it. However, since I wanted to teach, I had to get over the fear to be successful. But even with teaching experience, I was still uncomfortable speaking to an audience outside the classroom. Eventually I challenged myself by volunteering to speak at larger events and felt satisfied with accomplishing that. But there was one more speaking challenge I wanted to face, and that was to do comedy on stage in New York City at one of the improv comedy clubs.

I enjoy telling jokes in social situations and even came up with a few original jokes. I was getting some laughs at them among friends, so I decided to submit them to *Reader's Digest*. In case you don't know, *Reader's Digest* is a family-oriented magazine that shares stories, advice, and jokes. I submitted three jokes, and they contacted me to let me know they selected one for the magazine and sent me a check for $25. I was absolutely delighted as I had no idea I would hear from them. I'll take this opportunity to share the joke as follows:

> *"I finally make enough money to put a television in each room of my home. I live in a studio apartment."*

Once I had a few original jokes, one that made it to publication, I decided it was time to take on the challenge of performing comedy on a stage. I did improv twice with five-minute sessions each. While some jokes got laughs, others didn't. Trying to keep your cool when people aren't laughing is difficult, but I did it and I was comfortable with the outcome. For me, the goal wasn't about making people laugh, although any laughter felt good. Instead, it was about feeling empowered enough to take on such a scary challenge. It didn't matter if I succeeded or not. What mattered is that I wanted to give something a try and I was confident enough to do it. My hope is that by reading this book will help you feel the same way.

Challenge yourself and don't worry about failure. Learn to be comfortable with failing. We can't be good at everything. The experience you will get from both failure and success will enrich your life.

I may try comedy improv again, only this time I have experience and I'm able to analyze why some jokes fell flat to change my approach and give it another try. I find it fun to think things out and try to figure out a way to succeed. It's good exercise for the mind.

The lesson I am trying to put forth is for you to find activities and challenges that help you towards developing self-esteem for a confident and fulfilling life. Pursue interests and learn about your weaknesses and strengths. Determining what you do not like will naturally lead you to what you do like. The more you do, the closer you will get to finding your purpose and happiness in life.

So don't sit on the sidelines watching everyone else succeed. Try different things until you find interests and strengths that help build your self-esteem and confidence. Understanding the importance of this will lead you to continued success, peace, and happiness. So, "find your game" and prepare to launch toward success and great rewards.

Chapter 2

Learn How You Learn

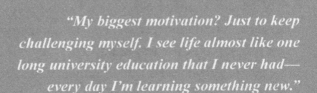

"My biggest motivation? Just to keep challenging myself. I see life almost like one long university education that I never had— every day I'm learning something new."

—RICHARD BRANSON

▩ Learning Strategies

Richard Branson is dyslexic and found studying difficult, so he dropped out of high school. But he used his intelligence and ambition to start the first of his many businesses, a magazine, at the age of sixteen. From there he moved on to many other business ventures to become a self-made billionaire.

David Neeleman suffered from attention-deficit/hyperactivity disorder (ADHD) which caused him great challenges in learning. So he decided to drop out of college to focus on his entrepreneurial desires and became the founder of JetBlue Airways.

Diane Swonk suffers from dyslexia and has difficulty remembering numbers. For example, she is unable to remember her pin and phone numbers. She suffered a great deal of humiliation and isolation while growing up, but she didn't "sit the bench." She went on to become a leading economist and author.

My reasoning in providing the above examples is not to dismiss the importance of school, but to rather convince you to persevere no matter the difficulty you are having with formal education. After doing your best to study and yet find you are still failing can be very discouraging. But that doesn't mean you can't succeed another way. Just because most people can do well with common formal education doesn't mean it's for everyone. Sometimes we just need to do our own thing to succeed.

When I was in middle and high school, I was able to follow classroom instruction and do well if I did my homework. But in college my anxiety got in the way of my learning. I had difficulty listening to the teacher and realized I wasn't going to learn that way. So I studied hard outside of class. I had to teach myself. I did the work necessary on my own to pass my courses. I needed quietness for me to study as I was easily disturbed by noise. I spent a lot of time in various libraries in town. I found that Wesleyan University's library in Middletown, Connecticut, provided the best place for me to study even though I didn't attend there. I didn't know anybody there, so I wasn't disturbed by friends and there were many rooms in the library for me to find the exact atmosphere I needed to concentrate.

I am pretty good at math but not as good with reading retention. On the other hand, I have a very intelligent friend who is superb at reading retention but not so good with math, the opposite of me. All of us have minds that are different, so we need to understand our strengths and weaknesses to plan our studies and life accordingly. For example, since I'm strong in math and like numbers, math related employment such as finance, accounting, and data analytics are good paths for me to pursue. But that doesn't mean I should ignore jobs that require reading retention like attorneys and publishers. It only means that if I want to pursue such career opportunities, I will need to develop ways to improve retaining what I read. One way I accomplished this was to make an outline of everything I read. Sure, it's extra work but sometimes we need to put in effort to reach our goals. While others can reach their goals in a straight line, we may have to zigzag to get reach ours. But if we truly want something, it's worth it.

At college I quickly got bored with reading assignments, so it was very difficult to pay attention to what I was reading. If I was going to pass my classes, I had to figure out a way to make the reading more interesting and improve on retention. I came up with the idea of going directly to the back of each chapter to the exercise questions. Then I worked to find the answers to each question in the chapter. I did this even though the exercise questions were not assigned. This helped make the reading much more interesting as well as helped me retain the information by writing down the answers. I have since suggested my students do the same thing if they were having difficulty with reading the chapters. I suggested it for not just my class, but for all other classes they take as well. After taking my suggestion they let me know it was a big help for them.

The internet provides unlimited resources to go beyond assigned reading to learn more. You have the ability to extend your understanding of the subject matter easily by doing a quick search using Google. There you will find other articles and videos to expand on your understanding of the material.

I suffer from ADHD so I find I am much better at teaching myself as opposed to listening to an instructor. It is difficult for me to keep my mind on the instructor's lecture because I'm easily bored and my mind wanders. To help overcome this fault I started to sit in the front row of each class. My mind would still wander, but in front of the class it occurred less often. If I sat in the back row, I got very little out of the lecture. Sitting in front with the teacher a few feet away from me kept me more engaged. So, at the start of every semester I made sure I got to class early to designate one of the front seats in each class for me. This may help you as well.

Another helpful method for learning is to take the lecture and reading material and act as if you are going to teach someone on the subject. They say the best way to learn is to teach. I couldn't agree more as I have memorized material more easily preparing to teach a class as opposed to just studying it to pass a test. That's because it forces me to take material and put it in my own words to explain it to others. So, if you want to do well on exams, create an outline of the material and prepare as if you are going to explain the material to your classmates or for a presentation. This takes time and extra work, of course. But if you want to reach a high grade point average you will need to do whatever it takes and avoid shortcuts that will keep you from strong grades.

After each class try taking time to think about the lecture while the subject matter is still fresh. You will do yourself a great service if you schedule time between classes to review the material the teacher lectured on. I used to schedule study time in between classes so that I could either write down notes or work on homework while the material was still fresh. This was a big help for my reading and lecture retention.

It's also important to talk about subject matter with fellow students. One way to do this is to form a study group. I did this in my last year of college and it was a big step towards my grade improvement. We met a couple times a week and while we talked about other things outside the courses, we mainly focused on course materials. We got to share our understanding as well as strategize on how to pass the tests. Quite often the other students discussed things I didn't consider so it was a wonderful way to ensure I got everything I needed to pass the courses with good grades.

Because I work in the corporate world as well as teach data analytics, I can provide real work content to learn from in my courses which greatly benefits students, especially for interviews because of the knowledge they learn about the working environment. I recall a time when I presented students with a real world example from the workplace involving a technical project. It was an interesting and fun class, and the students thoroughly enjoyed my lecture that day and thanked me for going beyond the standard class material. But as soon as I was done presenting, I saw each student take out their phones and do whatever it is they do on their phones—texting, listening to music, watching videos, etc. I thought about this for a minute and then I asked for their attention to discuss my observation. I explained that while technology is great, it can be a distraction to learning. Rather than discussing the demonstration I had just provided or asking me questions for more clarification, the students were anxious to get to their phones. Since they were not thinking about the lecture, they would soon forget what I just covered. The bottom line is that if you don't think about content, it will be difficult to recall it later. So be mindful that after each class you should give some thought to the lecture to help you retain the information.

Learning Styles

To do your best either in school or professionally, you will need to find your learning style. I'm more kinesthetic and solitary. I enjoy project work as opposed to studying and memorizing for tests. But if the teacher is requiring memorization for tests, I turn it into a project by creating notes or short books to help me retain the information. Do whatever it takes to get through the class with good grades. A list of some learning styles to help you determine which you identify most with is as follows:

1. **Visual** - Visual learners are stimulated by various types of images such as pictures, graphs, or flowcharts. They are able to digest the material more easily by seeing it as opposed to hearing it.

    My first book is a database design and programming book. I made it a point to put many pictures in the book to learn from as the reader reads through the material. I wrote the book with limited written information on each page to avoid overwhelming the reader. I wanted to make sure the reader understood the content before turning to the next page. Pictures helped enforce the material by showing examples of the written material.

Popular reporting tools incorporate visual graphs for managers to obtain information. The visuals quickly provide information that would take longer to absorb if it were written instead. For example, a bar chart quickly shows outcomes of comparisons as opposed to looking at numbers on a spreadsheet.

2. **Kinesthetic** - Kinesthetic learners like performing or doing things physically and being actively engaged. For example, instead of reading about how volcanoes erupt, the kinesthetic learner would learn best creating a volcano for a science project.

   Studying by creating a presentation of the material would help the kinesthetic learner. For example, using PowerPoint to create a presentation with pictures has the learner performing as opposed to reading.

3. **Aural** - The aural learner likes to have discussions about topics when learning. They enjoy hearing others and speaking answers. Rather than take notes, aural learners like listening to lectures.

Attending presentations outside the classroom would benefit the aural learner. There are many presentations one can find on YouTube to learn by as well.

4. **Social** - The social learner thrives on being around people. They enjoy working in groups, sharing their knowledge as well as listening to others speak.

    A study group is a good option for the social learner. Each member of the group shares their knowledge of the material giving the social learner the ideal scenario for learning.

5. **Solitary** - Solitary learners are self-motivated and prefer to learn on their own. They may find working with others distracting so they tend to work independently.

    Solitary learners can be found at home without distractions or in a library which provides the quiet atmosphere needed for learning.

6. **Verbal** - Verbal learners like reading and writing activities as well as listening. They enjoy taking notes which helps them to remember things. They also tend to like work play and rhymes.

    Attending or viewing presentations on video are helpful for the verbal learner. Creating presentations might be beneficial as well.

7. **Logical** - Logical learners like to learn by using orders, steps, and patterns. They tend to like math and computer programming.

I often tell students to do things in baby steps to avoid being overwhelmed. Logically building up to the ultimate goal helps logical learners best.

🔖 Grades

Good grades are very important, especially when you are first out of school. Since students often lack work experience, grades are what employers use for evaluation. The better your grades, the more opportunities you will have for employment after college. In addition, I have seen many young graduates who have 3.2 and above grade point averages enter early career mentoring programs at large corporations like Cigna Healthcare, United Healthcare, and Pratt & Whitney. It doesn't take long for these graduates to climb the ladder and become managers, directors, and above. They did the schoolwork to qualify for the mentoring programs and now reap the benefits.

Students with grade point averages lower than 3.2 will find it more challenging to find jobs and when they do those jobs are not as opportunistic. But that can be turned around. It's never too late to make a change for the better if you are willing. It's just a longer path.

My methodology was to always study hard enough for the A so that the least I would get would be a B. That has always worked for me with many times achieving an A or A minus. But when I didn't get an A, I ended up with a B. Certainly there were times when I got below a B, but it was rare, and it wasn't because of lack of studying. I always put in my best effort.

We now live in an age of endless resources to learn from. I work in technology so one of my favorite places to learn is from YouTube. YouTube provides numerous videos to learn from. Unlike a lecture, I can stop them while I try content out on my computer. Often I need to review parts of the video so I can easily reverse the video and continue at my own pace. YouTube is also a good place to learn math. My job requires that I work with statistics, so I often use YouTube to lean various formulas.

As mentioned earlier, there are several sources for research on the internet and you will need to take advantage of it at your job. Before asking a co-worker how to do something such as create a formula in Excel, you will be expected to learn it on your own from the internet. Asking questions of your co-workers that are easily found on the internet might make people think you are lazy which isn't good at review time. So, get used to being independent and finding answers on your own if you can.

When I have students working on assignments in class, I will be asked questions on how to do something. I explain I am willing to answer and help but only after the student has tried to figure it out on their own by searching the internet. This helps students learn to become more independent as well as improve their searching skills. Also, students will learn more from the research as opposed to me giving them the answer. The more you can do on your own to learn the better you will be for it.

❦ Embrace School

You should develop strong study habits and stick to them. Your studies need to take a priority above sports, social life, and dating. You are building a foundation for growth into adulthood so the stronger that foundation is, the better prepared for challenges later in life that will come your way.

Learn to embrace school and find a desire to do well. I didn't go back for my master's degree until I was age forty-two. I never thought I would pursue a master's degree, but if I wanted to teach, I needed to get one. I dreaded the idea of going back at first. But once I accepted that it was necessary to reach my goal of becoming a teacher, I embraced it and made it a priority in my life. I developed a desire to see it all the way through. Try to do the same with your schooling.

You should also try to build a relationship with your teachers. Your teachers are doing a job to teach students, so they find it rewarding when students are engaged in their classes. Quite often class participation will make up part of your grade and that has a subjective element to it. It's easier for a teacher to grade you on class participation if he/she knows you. It may result in an extra point or two to move your grade up to an A.

I want to share a humorous story regarding building a relationship with your teachers. While pursuing my master's degree I had a professor I will call Dr. Mary. She was strict and not very flexible when grading. I found time to talk to her after class and let her know that my goal was to teach and asked her for advice, which she gladly shared. I told her that I was working in the industry, so her course was in line with what I was doing. She appreciated that.

One day we received our tests back and I noticed I was deducted 5 points for a foolish mistake. It was obvious that I knew the material but somehow I answered incorrectly by marking the wrong area on the test. So, from my seat in front of the class and with the whole class listening I said, "Dr. Mary, you are looking quite angelic today." She got a laugh out of it along with the students in the class and she knew I was trying to convince her to give me the points. She agreed with me that it was a foolish mistake and gave me 2.5 points instead of 5. That was fair. I believe it was because I put in the effort to build a relationship with her that she did that for me. Of course, getting her to smile probably helped too.

Another method I used to build a relationship with professors was to research their backgrounds and then have a discussion with them about their achievements. It really helped me feel engaged at school and the relationships I built are still intact today.

Take your education seriously as it is the foundation for great achievements throughout life. Your goal should be to find out how you learn best and use those strategies to excel in your classes. Embrace school rather than dread it. Find a way to enjoy it. It is a small percentage of time when compared to the rest of your life and doing the hard work in the beginning will make challenges later in life easier to manage. Of course, your achievements in school will do wonders for your self-esteem.

Chapter 3

Avoid Victim Mentality

"In the long run, we shape our lives, and we shape ourselves. The process never ends until we die. And the choices we make are ultimately our own responsibility."

—ELEANOR ROOSEVELT

Many people are victims to past events in life that can affect personal and professional development. For example, many children and young adults have suffered greatly with traumatic experiences including physical, mental, and sexual abuse. The effects from these experiences can be devastating and affect personal growth well into adulthood. Poverty, bullying, rejection, and disabilities can also affect personal growth and lead to low self-esteem and lack of motivation. But while many of us may have been victimized with various experiences, it is up to us whether we carry on with a victim mentality. Dwelling on negative experiences will prevent us from developing prosperous and successful lives.

Victim Mentality Traits

Victim mentality is not inherited, but rather developed through negative experiences from our past. People who feel victimized often feel they don't have control over events in their lives. They tend to use their past negative experiences as excuses for not moving forward resulting in anger, depression, and lack of success. Luckily, if we are willing, we can overcome our victim mindsets to empower ourselves toward growth and success.

I'm not suggesting that we completely forget negative experiences from our past. After all, they are part of our lives. But it's important to keep in mind that negative circumstances don't define us. If you can, become a survivor from those experiences to develop, learn, and empower yourself to move forward toward a rewarding life.

It is important to recognize signs of victim mentality that people may be experiencing. Some of the more common signs are as follows:

1. **Anger** - People may spend their lives angry for no justifiable reason. Whatever happened in the past is still affecting them emotionally and they feel justified to be angry. This can have a very unproductive effect on relationships because anger can cause us to have irrational negative thoughts about other people.

   If you feel you have an angry personality you should avoid justifying or rationalizing the anger and, instead, work towards not allowing your past experiences to hinder your personality and future. Empower yourself with positive thoughts and you will find positive things will naturally come your way.

2. **Entitlement and fairness** - It can be frustrating seeing your peers going through life with easier circumstances. From my own experience, I used to think about how much easier other students had it than me with parents buying them cars, paying for their education, and sending them on vacations.

Dwelling on the fortune of my peers and how unfair it was to me did absolutely nothing for my forward progress. I learned to accept that I will experience challenges that are tougher than others. In the same sense, there are people less fortunate than me who will have tougher challenges. I realized I have energy and intelligence and those are two wonderful traits to move forward and reach my goals with. So, let's learn to empower ourselves toward success by taking on our challenges and not dwell on the fortunes of others.

3. **Limiting beliefs and self-destructing thoughts** - It is quite common to experience negative thoughts about ourselves. These thoughts can make us overly concerned about what others think of us and incorrectly believe it's something negative. It is important to control negative thoughts by doing things that make you feel good and replace negative thoughts with the positiveness in your life. The more you practice doing this, the more natural and instinctive it becomes.

As an example, a few years ago I accepted a part-time teaching position at Columbia University and was invited to a party to welcome the new teachers. While I am a very social person, I was having a difficult time trying to mingle with the full-time professors. It was as if they had no interest in talking to me at all. Because I learned to empower myself with positive thoughts, I didn't let this bother me. I simply went back to my table and talked with some people there, ate, and left in a good mood. I felt proud that I was invited to a dinner at Columbia University and didn't let the inability to socialize with the full-time professors ruin my evening. Stay positive and you will find life is quite wonderful because you are quite wonderful.

4. **Feeling sorry for yourself** - While feeling sorry for yourself might give you some relief from a negative situation, it is not empowering. Instead, it feeds the feeling of hopelessness and exaggerates the situation making it worse than it really is.

   If you are feeling down because of something that happened, it's okay to mourn it a bit, but you shouldn't allow it to stunt your progress. If you are feeling depressed, get some exercise, watch a good movie, talk to friends, play with your pet, or go eat something tasty. Change your mood and stay empowered. You are responsible for how you feel and no one else.

5. **Socializing with people who complain about their lives** - As the saying goes, "Misery loves company." Certainly, when we experience something negative we don't want to feel alone in our grief, so

we tend to socialize with others in similar situations. There are several support groups that serve this purpose. But if you find yourself spending more time with people who complain rather than people who inspire, this will tend to impede your growth.

I experienced a group of friends who were not experiencing success in life and seemed to lack direction, motivation, or both. They had each other to avoid loneliness, but they weren't happy. They wanted something more in life but did not know how to pursue it. They often criticized one another and never seemed to praise each other. If one of them did something positive, he received criticism instead of praise. It seemed because they weren't succeeding, they didn't want their friends to succeed either.

Try to recognize those who live their lives as complainers and lack motivation. They will tend to draw positive energy away from you. As you succeed you will find you have less in common with people like this. They want to talk negatively but your positive outcomes will have no place in their conversation.

Certainly, you may be struggling with something like finding a job, for example, and it might feel better to talk with others who are experiencing the same thing as opposed to others who are gainfully employed. While it can be therapeutic to discuss your struggles, you can also ask for advice on strategies to finding a job or offering strategies yourself. This is very different from just complaining. Keep your hope up and think about ways to reach your goals no matter the struggle.

Overcoming Victim Mentality

If you find you are experiencing traits of victim mentality, you can overcome it with practicing the following simple lessons below:

1. **Focus on your gains** - When you make gains in your personal life reward yourself by doing something special and reflect on it often. The goal is to change your mindset to think about the positives and not the negatives. So go out and have a nice dinner, buy a new clothing item, or share your experience with someone. Celebrate your achievements.

2. **Avoid negative energy** - It makes no sense to be around negative situations if you can avoid it. Avoid arguments and stressful events, especially if they don't provide any value to your life. Socialize with friends that are inspirational rather than complainers.

   I have learned to avoid situations that invite negative conversations. For example, politics is a very emotional subject and should be avoided. To avoid such conversations, I simply make up a reason to excuse myself and move on.

3. **Be grateful** - If you stop and think about it, I think you will find many reasons to be grateful, especially when compared to people less fortunate. If you have warm friends and family, that is something to be grateful for. If you are in school, that is another thing to be grateful for. If your life is moving forward, well, then, you have a lot to be grateful about.

   I have learned to be grateful for the smallest of things in my life. As I walk around my housing community, I enjoy greeting the dogs that are so happy to meet me. Watching them pull their owners toward me while wagging their tails makes me feel very warm inside.

   Also, talking and joking with people in the neighborhood and helping neighbors when I can makes me feel like I belong to a family. We hold parties and watch out for one another, so I am very grateful for that.

It's Up to You

I know many people who have overcome serious challenges. If they wanted to, they could use their circumstances for pity and explanation for lack of success. Sometimes our upbringing programs us to think that we are powerless over challenging circumstances but it's not true. We don't have to resort to being a product of our environment when there is little or no value to it. You have the power to determine your fate. You can either give in to your circumstances or choose to learn from them and continue forward. Challenges are an opportunity to learn, grow, and become stronger because of the circumstances and not lose faith in our ability to pursue our goals. I truly believe we all have a purpose in life. Continue your journey to find yours.

We all know people who are lucky by having families that provide financial support toward their goals. You may not be so lucky, but you shouldn't let that stop you. You shouldn't play victim and let limited finances be the reason for not chasing after a dream. If your dream is to finish college, then figure out a way to come up with the money to do so. I always found truth in the following proverb:

"Where there's a will, there's a way."

I have tried to live life that way. If I was WILLING to put in the effort toward a goal, I could do it, no matter the challenges that laid before me. If it's important enough, and you are willing, you can achieve what you want. But the will must be there.

I've come to know many people who have had and still have significant difficulties in life but have chosen to move forward despite them. One person that comes to mind is someone I know from grade school and then later in college. I will call him Mike (not his real name). He was born without arms but didn't let that stop him from experiencing life like everyone else. I'm sure you can imagine that not having arms makes the simplest of things, like opening a door or eating independently, challenging compared to the rest of us with arms. Yet I saw Mike use his feet to type at a computer, eat sandwiches, write, and even drive a car. He had a lot of friends, excelled at school, and went on to a successful career in computer science. I never witnessed Mike depressed. In class he sat in the front row and engaged in classroom discussion. Outside of class, he socialized with classmates and had a good time. He was a joy to be around.

Then there are people I know who suffered emotional and physical abuse as children but worked their way through it to become successful adults. Some sought professional help to overcome the nightmare of their experiences. It's not easy, the past will always be there, but they didn't let it impede their drive to reach their goals.

Overcoming Adversity

It's important to understand that it's okay to seek help when you need it to overcome challenges. Many successful people do. I did as well. Talk to a teacher, pastor, family member, friend or seek professional help if necessary to assist you through your situations. But don't let challenges dissuade you from your accomplishing your goals. Get the help you need to continue on your path towards your dreams.

There are several well-known people who faced adversity in their lives, but they kept their focus on their dreams and were able to overcome them. They chose between drowning in their circumstances or moving forward to fulfil their purpose in life. Below are a few of the people you may be familiar with.

1. **Jim Carrey** - Jim Carrey dropped out of school at age fifteen to help support his homeless family. He was determined to become a comedian and did not let his circumstances get in the way. In 1987 he moved from Canada to Los Angeles to pursue his dreams of becoming a comedian and actor. He was penniless but he didn't let that stop him. He practiced affirmations by visualizing what he wanted for himself.

    In 1992 Carrey wrote a check for ten million dollars and dated it three years in advanced for Thanksgiving Day 1995. Around that time Carrey received a ten-million-dollar check for his work on the movie *Dumb and Dumber.*

2. **Bethany Hamilton** - At the age of thirteen Bethany Hamilton lost her arm to a shark while surfing and almost died. Her dream was to become a professional surfer and she didn't let the loss of an arm stop her.

    Twenty-six days after the shark attack she started to learn to become a one-armed surfer and went on to win many professional events as a professional surfer.

3. **Richard Branson** - Richard Branson was born dyslexic and found school challenging because of it. While he did poorly in school, he was determined to succeed in life and follow his dreams to become a successful entrepreneur. Along the way he had many failures but learned to overcome them. He is quoted as saying:

> "Failure is a wonderful way of learning, as an entrepreneur, if you're not taking risks, you're not going to achieve anything... I've learned the hard way sometimes."

Today Branson is owner of airlines, record labels, radio stations, hotels, and other companies. He is worth over five billion dollars.

4. **Stephen King** - Stephen King's first novel was rejected thirty times and he almost gave up. His wife convinced him to continue trying which resulted in him becoming a successful author with over 350 million books sold.

5. **Kris Carr** - In 2003, Kris Carr was thirty-two years old when she was diagnosed with a rare and incurable stage IV cancer. But rather than giving in to

this challenge, she decided to take it on and began a nutritional lifestyle that helped her survive and become a successful author sharing her knowledge of nutrition and lifestyle.

6. **Abraham Lincoln** - When ranking presidents of the United States, President Abraham Lincoln ranks as the highest. Yet, before becoming president, Lincoln faced many difficult challenges. He was born into poverty, lacked formal education, lost is first love at age twenty-six, failed in business twice and lost in multiple political races. But quite possibly his biggest challenge was suffering from clinical depression, even contemplating suicide. Despite his challenges, he kept on his path toward his goals to become the sixteenth president of the United States.

The following letter is from the Collected Works of Abraham Lincoln, Volume 5. It is a letter to Quintin Campbell, a West Point cadet who was feeling discouraged. His mother, a relative of President Lincoln's wife, Mary, wrote President Lincoln to ask him reach out to her son.

> *"Your good mother tells me you are feeling very badly in your new situation. Allow me to assure you it is a perfect certainty that you will, very soon, feel better—quite happy—if you only stick to the resolution you have taken*

> *to procure a military education. I am older*
> *than you, have felt badly myself, and know,*
> *what I tell you is true. Adhere to your purpose*
> *and you will soon feel as well as you ever did.*
> *On the contrary, if you falter, and give up,*
> *you will lose the power of keeping any resolu-*
> *tion, and will regret it all your life. Take the*
> *advice of a friend, who, though he never saw*
> *you, deeply sympathizes with you, and stick*
> *to your purpose.*
> *Sincerely your friend,*
> *A. LINCOLN"*

7. **Oprah Winfrey** - Oprah Winfrey grew up in poverty and was sexually abused by relatives resulting in pregnancy and followed by a miscarriage. But she was determined to make something of herself and has become one of the most influential people ever. She became the first black female billionaire and donates time and money toward multiple organizations.

8. **Stephen Hawking** - Stephen Hawking spent his adult life suffering with amyotrophic lateral sclerosis (ALS), a neurological disease that affects muscles and inhibits physical function. When he was diagnosed at age twenty-one with the disease, doctors didn't give him more than a year to live. But he

lived until age seventy-six and used his mind and determination to write fifteen books on physics, astronomy, and the universe. He is quoted as saying:

> *"Look up at the stars and not down at your feet. Try to make sense of what you see and wonder about what makes the universe exist."*
> *"Be curious."*

9. **Malala Yousafzai** - At age eleven, Malala Yousafzai started fighting for the right of every child to receive an education, especially girls, despite the Taliban threats to kill her. At age fifteen she was shot in the head and was seriously wounded but survived. After recovering she had to escape to England and live in exile. At age seventeen she wrote a memoir on her life that became an international best seller. Also at age seventeen, she became the youngest recipient of the Nobel Peace Prize.

10. **Sylvester Stallone** - Sylvester Stallone grew up in poverty and had a speech impairment due to forceps used at birth damaging nerves and causing paralysis around his mouth. He was mocked for the way he talked but was determined to become an actor. At one time, he was so poor he had to sell his dog for twenty-five dollars. But he continued to pursue his dreams and wrote the script for Rocky.

While the producers liked the script for Rocky, they didn't want Stallone to star in it. However, Stallone wouldn't sell the script unless he was the main character, even though he had no money. He eventually got what he wanted and became an international superstar as actor, writer, and director.

All the people mentioned above had at least one characteristic in common, resilience. They all had the determination to adapt to their challenging experiences and continue their path forward. If we are willing, we can find our inner resiliency and overcome obstacles by accepting the challenges and finding other ways to reach our desires. None of the examples mentioned reached success the first time around and chances are you won't either. But that shouldn't discourage you. Instead take what you have learned from the experiences and move on.

Do what you need to overcome the adversities in your life. To move forward and succeed do not succumb to a victim mentality. Instead, accept the challenges life sends you, focus, strategize, and continue to work towards your goals. Remember, you are in charge of your life so empower yourself to live your life to its fullest.

I will end this chapter with the following quote from Charles Stanley, Sr., pastor of First Baptist Church in Atlanta.

> *"Disappointments are inevitable;*
> *discouragement is a choice."*

Chapter 4

Becoming Independent

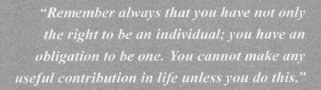

"Remember always that you have not only the right to be an individual; you have an obligation to be one. You cannot make any useful contribution in life unless you do this."

—ELEANOR ROOSEVELT

Take Responsibility for Yourself

If you are in high school or college, you should start thinking about what it takes to live independently. Being truly independent will help you develop your self-esteem and provide the confidence you will need to take on challenges throughout your life.

It doesn't matter if you are in high school, college, or employed full-time, there are steps you can take toward your independence. Below I've broken down steps you can take to gain independence in three different categories.

High School

1. **Grades** - Your parents shouldn't have to tell you to do your homework. Your homework and grades are your responsibility. This means developing disciplined study habits to be in control of your grades. Make sure you dedicate sufficient time for doing your homework when you still have energy to think. You will need to have a place in the home to study without interruption. If you don't, have a discussion with your parents about finding a place or go to the library. Your studies should take priority over sports and social activities. Keep in mind that high school is preparation for college so do all you can to make sure you are prepared.

2. **Tidiness** - Many young men and women have joined the military and as part of their responsibilities learned to be tidy as a requirement. You don't have to join the military to do the same thing. If you have been given a room of your own, that's a privilege and it's your responsibility to keep it clean. Before you leave the house make sure your bed is made and tidy up your room. Be proud of your room and make it a representation of your personality.

    The same discipline should be applied to your clothing. Make sure your clothes are clean and neat before leaving the house.

3. **Help around the house** - You don't need to wait for your parents to ask you for help. Look around and see how you can contribute. Volunteer to do laundry, dishes, clean the house, or do yard work. I'm sure the more you take on responsibility and act like an adult, the more your parents will treat you like one.

4. **Get your driver's license** - Milestones are key life events we experience as we grow to become independent adults. One of those events is getting your driver's license as it is essential for independence. Once you turn age sixteen make it a goal to get you driver's license, even if you don't have

a car to drive. I didn't have a car available to me, but I pursued my driver's license anyway by going to driving school. Many young people have done the same thing.

Getting your driver's license is a goal that should be reached as close as possible to age sixteen because other events like college and work responsibilities will be a top concern a couple of years later. Having your driver's license is one less thing to think about.

5. **Finding your interests** - If you haven't done so already, high school is a good time to start finding your interests and learning what you are good at. This will help you make decisions for your future in college and employment. It will help you build a social circle by finding compatible friends.

6. **Find a job** - As long as your studies are not sacrificed, I suggest finding a job. If a job would get in the way of your studies, then you can always get a job during the summer months when school is out. A job will teach you employment responsibilities as well as introduce you to money management. Before graduating high school, you should learn how to budget your money for savings, entertainment, and expenses like clothes. Money management will follow you the rest of your life.

College

7. **Plan your own appointments** - I was talking with someone's mother not too long ago who was still planning dentist appointments for her twenty-two-year-old daughter. Another mother I know has a son who is a tennis pro at age twenty-seven and called him to make sure he's drinking enough water on hot days. Even if your parents want to treat you the same way, don't allow it to happen. You cannot become independent and responsible relying on your parents to make sure your necessities are covered. Certainly, you can still consult your parents for guidance, but take responsibility of your appointments.

8. **Money responsibilities** - You will need to manage your expenses while in college. There is the expense of college, books, clothes, social activities, and maybe even cars and insurance. It is good experience balancing all these expenses, not to mention the responsible thing to do. If your parents are paying these expenses, I suggest you at least take an interest in how your parents are managing it all for you. First, you should be thankful they are managing the expenses for you. Second, get involved by asking them about the budget and learning how they do it. Also, don't surprise them at the last minute with expenses.

College usually has opportunities for student workers. This would be good for you to take on some responsibility of expenses, even if it was for your entertainment.

9. **Try doing things alone** - Many young people are uncomfortable doing things alone. This can include shopping, doctors' appointments, hair appointments, or even appointments with the motor vehicle department. They feel more comfortable with a parent or friend joining them. The more you do alone, the more confidence you will gain and independent you will feel.

When deciding to do things alone, safety comes first. Make sure whatever you plan on doing alone, you are safe doing it. For example, parking garages can be dangerous, especially for women. So, if you need to bring someone with you for safety reasons, then do so.

Employment

10. **Prepare to leave home** - To become truly independent, you will need to move out on your own. But before doing so, take the time to plan your budget as living on your own is expensive and there are many expenses you may not have thought of. Some

suggestions to help plan your big step to independent living are listed below:

a. Determine what you can afford for a monthly rent.
b. Determine location and apartment size.
c. Plan a budget for rent/mortgage, utilities, home insurance, cable, cell phone, and food.
d. Save for your initial home costs such as furniture, kitchen items, bathroom items, and cleaning items.
e. Plan your move accordingly as you may need some time to settle. Perhaps a couple of days off work will help you.

11. **Learn more about you** - Living independently provides a wonderful opportunity to learn more about yourself. Take this time to experience different things, meet new people, go on trips, and set up short and long term goals. Independent living is very empowering and will add to your self-esteem.

Choosing a Career

Quite often my students ask me how I chose a career in computer science and how I knew I would like it. Those are great questions and important ones too. But I don't think they expect my answers. I explain I didn't know I would like computer science. I chose a career in computer science because I heard it was a promising career and I needed to become financially independent, so I learned to like it. My priority was to become independent because I had to. There was no one to lean on for help. I was lucky that I had the capacity to learn computer science. Not everyone is able to, just like some people are good at math and others are not. I saw I was able to learn computer science, so I stuck with it, and it was a good career path to pursue financial independence. Once my financial independence was in place, I could focus on making life more pleasurable, even changing careers.

I wouldn't choose computer science again. I found I have other interests that I enjoy much more, like education, finance, and project management. But I was the youngest of four children along with my twin, and the first to go to college. College was new to the family so there wasn't much guidance and I had to figure out what to do on my own. I was ignorant to choices and possibilities. But I set out to make a good living and I got that accomplished.

Years later I picked up a second career teaching and found that is my passion. I used my computer science education and industry experience to teach others on the same subject, so things really did turn out good for me and I am thankful.

Quite often, we are given the advice that we should pursue careers that interest us. I do agree this is good advice... to an extent. Many people have chosen career paths without thinking about whether the incomes associated with those careers will be enough to pay for an independent and prosperous living. You will have to think beyond what your interests are to consider the income potential to make sure you will be able to sustain yourself and provide a future. Unfortunately, many students have not considered this and spent time and money for an education or skill that doesn't earn enough for living expenses.

There are career coaches who suggest pursuing your interests and then learning to monetize them to make a living. Certainly, many people have had success with monetizing their interests. For example, people who enjoy building things have learned trades and become very successful at careers in carpentry, electrical, and construction. Many of those same people have become entrepreneurs and run their own businesses. Others have gone on to college to pursue professional careers like law, accounting, and computer engineering.

However, some people may find their interests are not so easy to monetize. For example, pursuing an interest in art or music is admirable, but being able to monetize it enough to live financially independent isn't so easy. There are some, of course, who were able to achieve financial success in art and music, but it is rare. I personally know music artists who have been struggling after more than ten years. They are exceptionally good musicians and even have successful recordings, but they are still struggling to make ends meet.

I know of people who have pursued acting careers but never got the big break to lead to financial independence and they never know where their next paycheck is coming from. When I worked on the Adam Sandler movie, *Grown Ups 2*, I met several actors who travel to accept small parts in movies. They seemed very content and they were fun to talk to, but they were struggling financially. For some people, living paycheck to paycheck is fine and they would rather enjoy their life that way rather than worry about their financial future. But if you have dreams of home ownership, spouse, family, and retirement, you will need to think about a more reliable source of income. You don't have to totally give up your interests as you can still pursue them in your spare time, as I do with teaching and authoring books.

As you get older you will find new goals and responsibilities in your life so you will want to make sure you have the financial resources to support them. For example, the great American dream of owning your own house may be something you desire in your future. Also, if you plan on having a family, it is a big responsibility requiring time and financial resources. You might want to add value to your life by planning pleasurable activities like travel, snowboarding, eating out, and concerts. If so, you will need a good income to support all this. Consider a timeline of when you want to reach your goals and the finances required to achieve and sustain those goals. Use a timeline management tool to help you strategize. A simple example is shown below.

Goal	Amount Required	Time Frame
Down payment for home	50,000.00 to 100,000.00	2027
Travel to Europe	5,000.00	2028
Pay off student loan	35,000.00	2030
Own business	25,000.00	2032

Your plans can change so don't think you need to follow the timeline you come up with exactly. Change it as needed. But it does provide you some degree of guidance and will help keep your mind focused. I have found that when I think about goals, they happen.

If money is less important and enjoying your interests is what you want to base your goals on, that's fine too, if you can support yourself. For example, if music is your passion and you want to prioritize your time on it, money may be less important. However, if independence is a goal, you will still need to pay for such things as shelter, food, car, and medical expenses. I've known people who are very happy living day by day and putting all their energy into their passion. But long term independent living will be a challenge, especially when you have not saved for a rainy day.

Whatever path you choose, I would hope that you choose one that provides independent living. Doing so is empowering and will help you find your true calling and build your self-esteem to accomplish more in life. I also think when we are capable adults, we should be responsible for ourselves and avoid relying on others.

If you want to continue to pursue interests that make little or no income, you can do so with a job that generates income and then when not at work you can continue with your passion. For example, I worked with many people in the corporate world that played in bands on the side. They were able to support their family while staying on top of their music at night and on weekends.

🐝 Money Management

It is important to understand money is a necessity for acquiring goods and the services required to live. Therefore, you will need to learn to manage it accordingly. To become truly independent, you will need to learn to earn, budget, and invest money.

For budgeting and managing my money, I use Microsoft Excel. Figure 1 demonstrates a fictitious example of what I set up to manage my checking account.

Check Number	Date	Transaction Description	Payment or Withdrawl	Deposit	Balance
		2022 Check Book			
	12/31/2021	Balance From 2021			2,933.02
	12/31/2021	January Mortgage	2,144.06		788.96
	12/31/2021	January Power and Light	75.20		713.76
	12/31/2021	January Cable	162.00		551.76
	12/31/2021	January Verizon Cell	85.00		466.76
	12/31/2021	January HOA Fees	183.88		282.88
	12/31/2021	January Water	4.71		278.17
	12/31/2021	January Car Payment	175.00		103.17
	1/5/2022	Pay Day		2,500.00	2,603.17
	1/5/2022	Savings	250.00		2,353.17
	1/8/2022	Cash for Entertainment	200.00		2,153.17
	1/15/2022	Payment to Credit Card	300.00		1,853.17
	1/19/2022	Pay Day		2,500.00	4,353.17
	1/19/2022	February Mortgage	2,144.06		2,209.11
	1/19/2022	February Florida Power and Light	75.20		2,133.91
	1/19/2022	February Cable Hotwire	162.00		1,971.91
	1/19/2022	February Verizon Cell	85.00		1,886.91
	1/19/2022	February HOA Fees	183.88		1,703.03
	1/19/2022	February Water	4.71		1,698.32
	1/19/2022	February Car Payment	175.00		1,523.32
	1/19/2022	Savings	500.00		1,023.32
257	1/19/2022	Payment for gym fees	225.00		798.32
	1/19/2022	Cash for Entertainment	200.00		598.32

Sheet1 Sheet2 Sheet3 ⊕

FIGURE 1

The first column contains the check number if I use checks. You can see on the second to the last line I entered the check number of 257 for paying the gym. The second column is the transaction date. The third column, Transaction Description, describes the transaction that took place. Notice I highlight specific rows with yellow. These are my monthly living expenses and I like having that stand out. Each month I pay for those expenses I copy from the previous month. So, you see the first highlighted group for January and the second for February.

Payment or Withdrawal is next, and it is a deduction from the balance on my checking account. For example, each of the living expenses is a deduction from my account. On December 31, 2021, there are several deductions related to living expenses. The first one is for the mortgage for $2,144.06 leaving a balance of $788.96

$$2,933.02 - 2,144.06 = 788.96$$

The next line item is for Power and Light for $75.20 resulting in a balance of $713.76.

$$788.96 - 75.20 = 713.76$$

The fifth column is Deposit which is the amount added to the checking account. On January 5, 2022, I got paid so that results in an addition to the checking account resulting in a balance of $2,603.17.

$$1,853.17 + 2500.00 = 2,603.17$$

The sixth and final column is the balance. This contains an excel formula to perform the additions and subtractions to automatically generate the balance. Teaching how to use Excel is beyond the scope of this book so if you are not familiar with it, you can quickly find learning videos on YouTube and other sites.

As you plan your goals, please include financial independence as one of your priorities. Generating a living income and learning proper money management will help you reach your goals and live a fulfilling life. Your self-esteem will benefit, and you will continue to find personal and professional growth opportunities.

Chapter 5

Choosing a College Major

"People often say that this or that person has not yet found himself. But the self is not something one finds; it is something one creates."

—THOMAS SZASZ, THE SECOND SIN

Choosing a college major can be one of the hardest choices a young person has to make. While we are in our teenage years, society expects us to know what we want to do with the rest of our lives when preparing to go to college. Making this decision can be very stressful and, often, leave students anxious and discouraged. To help alleviate the stress when choosing a major we should remember that college is more than training for a career. It is a place to learn about the world as well as about ourselves. It provides a place to mature into young adults and build self-esteem to face the world before us.

🞕 Considerations for Choosing a Major

1. **Interests** - Your first hint to choosing a major is determining your interests. Think about what you enjoy. For example, are you interested in science, math, drama, business, writing, etc.? Once you have considered possible interests ask yourself if you would like to teach the subject matter or work in the industry. For example, if you like math and teaching, then a major in education might be the right path for you. If you like the idea of a job using math, then perhaps engineering, accounting, or finance degrees are something to consider.

   Once you enter college your interests could change and that is both okay and common. We learn more of what interests us by socializing with other students and utilizing the resources colleges provide. So, no need to stress out about a change of interests. Remember, you are growing and growing means learning about new things, including new things about yourself.

2. **Capacities** - Consider your capacities when choosing a major. If writing is a strong skill for you, perhaps a degree in journalism would be a good fit. If you find that you have an inviting personality, maybe sales or leadership types of degrees would be good choices. Look for things that both come naturally to you and that you enjoy.

   Try to keep in mind that if something is too easy it might bore you. So make sure you enjoy what you do and not choose a degree path because it's easy.

3. **Explore** - When you are unsure of what you want to major in, many students spend their first semesters taking general studies courses which are required in any degree program. This allows them to take more time exploring possible majors with the help of meeting new friends and discussing college major choices. In addition, you can use the many college resources to open your mind to new interests.

4. **Department Advisors** - Talk to department advisors to learn more about majors you are considering. For example, learn what courses are required in each major program, possible advanced degrees, and career opportunities. Advisors can also connect you with other students who have chosen the degree program you are considering so that you can learn about it from a student's perspective.

5. **Employability and Salary** - When considering a major, you should consider available employment opportunities in the degree path you have chosen so that you can grow and support yourself. Consider income potential as well as career growth opportunities. For example, I know people who have studied nursing and once employed entered graduate school to become nursing practitioners.

   Whatever you decide on, do your due diligence in researching the job to make sure it fits what you like, as well as provides you with the means to make a living. Companies are always willing to talk to young adults inquiring about careers so don't be afraid to send them a letter or email to request a meeting with them to learn more about career opportunities and educational requirements.

🪶 Liberal Arts and General Studies

When I think about choosing a college major, I am re-minded of an experience I had working with a young man who was my realtor while looking for an apartment in New York City. I'll call him Jeff to avoid giving away his identity. I found Jeff to be a well-mannered twenty-four-year-old who was energetic and had a personality that made me feel comfortable immediately. He was very personable and we discussed many things, including his cultural background from Persia. He had taught me a lot about his culture so after looking at apartments, I thought it would be fun to ask him to join me for dinner so that we could continue our interesting conversations and he accepted.

Jeff seemed to be very educated and confident, so I assumed he went to college but wasn't sure, so I asked. He said that he had gone to college but dropped out because he could not pass the required math courses. I inquired and found that he majored in business administration and the math course requirements were beyond his ability, so he got discouraged and dropped out. I am unsure which college he had attended but the business administration curriculum there required courses in calculus.

I used this opportunity to help Jeff see college differ-ently. First, I wanted to make sure he understood I was very impressed with him, so I praised him on his communication skills and his attention to detail. Then I asked him how math courses could make that better. This, of course, was a rhetorical question so I didn't expect an answer. My point is that some curriculums put emphasis on subject matter that would have little or nothing to do with the career choice one has decided to pursue. Jeff was wonderful at his job and math would not help him get any better at it, but other courses would.

I explained that some of the most memorable and useful courses I had taken in college had little to do with my major in management information systems. Instead, they helped me understand the world and my life which then helped me toward reaching my goals. Courses in literature, history, and science opened my mind to things I never thought about. I had become educated about the world not because of my major, but because of the general education course choices that are included in degree programs.

I told Jeff that he should consider returning to college to pursue a major that does not require calculus courses. For example, a degree in liberal arts or general studies would provide a well-rounded and diversified education that would be inspirational and will help him converse on a wide range of topics. Since Jeff was interested in sales and real estate, his ability to have discussions on various topics would benefit him greatly with customer relationships.

In addition, a major in liberal arts or general studies can help students find what interests them most. After graduation, they may likely find they are better positioned to decide on the correct career path for them and pursue that either with employment, advanced studies, or both.

For many careers there is no choice, a specific degree is required. For example, careers in healthcare, engineering, law, and accounting require specific degrees. But for other careers, such as sales, public relations, and customer representative consultant, a degree in liberal arts or general studies will provide students with stronger communication skills, boost critical thinking methods, and offer students a broader range of knowledge in different subjects.

As you take your courses you will find that your mind becomes clearer to think about your interests and the path you would like to pursue to reach a promising professional and personal life.

It is not uncommon for many students to struggle through the advanced math courses in college. I did myself, even though I'm pretty good at math. I was a computer science major and there were four courses in calculus that were required. While I was good at computer programming, the required calculus courses were too difficult for me, and I found it was taking away study time from my other subjects, so my grades were suffering.

Since the calculus courses were affecting my other course grades, I had to give serious thought about making a change. There was another degree program called Management Information Systems, or MIS, that was also computer programming related but with emphasis on business knowledge and less on engineering. It required only one calculus course, so I switched majors. This change proved to be the right choice since my goal was to code business applications and I was able to improve my grade point average without all the calculous courses required in the computer science major.

▓ Choosing a College

There are many factors involved when choosing a college, so it is important to take the time to do your research and make an informed decision. I've listed some of the more important factors below to help guide you towards your decision.

1. **Finances** - Your financial position and ability to pay off student loans after graduation is something to be concerned about. Taking on too much debt can affect goals you have after graduation and later in life, so you need to balance cost against future earnings.

   To help minimize college expenses you can take advantage of the many scholarships and grants available to college students. Also, when trying to decide on which college to choose, weigh the expenses against educational value and career plans. For example, your first choice for a college may be more expensive than your second and third choices. You will need to determine if your first choice has enough added value to make it worth the extra money.

Some students choose to spend their first two years at a community college to save money and then transfer their credits to a four-year college or university. If you make this choice, you will need to make sure the college you plan on transferring to will accept the credits. Too many students have failed to confirm acceptance of the transfer of credits and ended up taking more classes than necessary to graduate.

2. **Commute or Dorms** - While commuting to college will save you money when living in your parents' home, commuters tend to miss out on many of the social activities that college campuses offer. Social activities are not only fun, but more importantly, they are very important in building your social capital which will serve you all your life. Many students have stayed in contact with people they met in college and that often turns into employment opportunities.

3. **Accreditation** - Accreditation ensures that colleges provide quality and respected education. Colleges enter associations of accreditation that are evaluated by its peers and gives the colleges credibility. There are six regional accreditations that you want to consider before choosing a college/university. They are as follow:

1. New England
2. Middle States
3. North Central
4. Southern
5. Western
6. Northwest

Accreditation means that the college/university follows high standards for education and the ability to receive financial aid for college is dependent on it.

4. **School Size** - For some, a large campus and classes is enticing while others are more comfortable with smaller classes and campuses. It's important that you choose a college that fits your comfort zone so that stress doesn't impede your studies. Schedule visits to the colleges before deciding to determine which college size and format fits you best.

5. **Online Versus On-Campus** - You have options for online colleges now and this may be convenient to your learning style as well as your lifestyle. However, there is value in social opportunities on campus so you may want to consider on campus if your situation allows it. There are also hybrid campuses so that you can participate in both online and on-campus courses.

▓ Deciding to Pursue a Degree

I like the idea of pursuing a bachelor's degree because it removes barriers to opportunities that may come later in life. For example, many employers won't consider candidates without a bachelor's degree even if they have ample work experience. I have a friend with decades of computer networking experience and, recently, he was questioned about not having a degree. I don't know if that was a factor in not being offered the job, but it may have been.

Another reason I like the idea of pursuing college is that it can help provide significant development towards your maturity, independence, social capital, and overall education. College exposes you to a lot of subject matter that you may never have considered on your own.

While college is not for everyone, learning is. I know very intelligent people without college degrees who did extremely well professionally and personally. It is up to us to educate ourselves formally through college, independently, or both. I believe one can educate themselves without college and do so more freely without the restrictions that formal education has. But society is partial to the college degree so it opens opportunities that may not occur otherwise.

Whatever you choose, please don't let challenges like difficult courses in math dissuade you from pursuing your goals. We all need to learn our strengths and capabilities to achieve success. If we can't reach our goals in a straight line, then we can zigzag towards them instead.

Chapter 6

Entrepreneurship

"I think people who have a real entrepreneurial spirit, who can face difficulties and overcome them, should absolutely follow their desires. It makes for a much more interesting life."

—MARTHA STEWART

Some of the most rewarding experiences I have ever had was owning my own businesses. I had a few of them. When I was younger someone gave me an idea to buy a used stump grinder as there was a need to grind stumps left over from trees that had fallen or were taken down. So, I took a chance and spent three thousand dollars on a used stump grinder. While I made a good amount of money grinding stumps, it was secondary to the experience I got from being an entrepreneur.

My First Business

Being an owner of a business gave me the freedom to use my mind in ways I never had. I found myself becoming more creative and strategic in my thinking. For example, I always found the thought of removing stumps a bit funny, so I came up with the business name "Stump Busters," a play off the movie title *Ghostbusters*. Then I designed a business card with an animated image that leant itself to mimic the *Ghostbusters* image. The idea of the name and image came to me while I was lying in bed thinking about the business. I created the image using CorelDRAW software.

I used the image for my business cards and that resulted in a customer seeing my business card and laughing so hard that it prompted her to hire me to grind her tree stumps. In addition, I put the image on magnetic signs that I attached to the doors of my truck resulting in people stopping me as I was driving by to ask me to come to their houses to grind their stumps. The image and name served as a wonderful promotional strategy that I would never have experienced working for someone else.

I learned how to increase business by placing ads in various newspapers (days before the internet) and hanging signs in shopping centers. I searched for tree removal companies that didn't have stump grinders and met with them to form partnerships where I sub-contracted my stump grinding services. They would bid on tree jobs, and we negotiated bids for the tree work combined with stump grinding to come up with a fair deal for everyone.

For smaller tree removals, I purchased chain saws so that I could do the whole job myself without requiring tree removal companies. My business grew fast. I also leveraged the business to perform landscaping services such as lawn maintenance and planting beds.

I learned how to bid on jobs of various sizes and came up with plans to beat my competitors. For example, I was losing bids to competitors even after lowering my prices. I had to think about it for a while but reached the conclusion I was losing bids to competitors because potential customers were sharing my bids with them. So, when customers called asking for bids, I suggested they get all their bids from my competitors first and I would then go over and beat their bids. When I did go to their home to give them a price, I did the job immediately to prevent them from seeking another bid. I never lost a job again to outbidding.

I learned that I was pretty good at selling to customers. I used to drive around and look for yards with stumps and "cold call" the customers by knocking on their doors. I quickly put into practice what I read about impulsive buyers. As soon as they agreed to my grinding their stumps, I learned to do it right then. Otherwise, if I planned it for another day, they sometimes changed their minds.

I oversaw everything, selling my services to customers, equipment and supply purchases, budgeting, insurance, sub-contracting, advertising, hiring help, and business strategies. It was a very empowering experience and helped provide the confidence and self-esteem needed for more successes later in life.

Unlike working for an employer where any mistake I made would hurt my bonuses or promotions months later, as a business owner I could make the appropriate corrections and get right back on track to being productive. Mistakes were learning lessons that led to improvement in business as opposed to negative evaluations with employers.

I thoroughly enjoyed running my own business and being in charge. I loved the independence to be creative and strategic and pursue opportunities that I would not experience working for someone. As the owner of a business,

I was responsible for everything and that helped me grow professionally and personally.

▓ Becoming An Author

I guess now, you can say, I've entered the book writing business since the book you are now reading is the second book I have authored. Like all new business ventures, there is a lot to learn. I knew very little about authoring a book when I started. My first book was an academic book titled *Introduction to Database Design and SQL*. I was inspired to write my first book because I found the available books written for college courses lacked vital information and skill learning needed for the industry. Since I work in the corporate environment, I can write and teach skills most sought after by employers. Of course, this helped students immensely during their interviews.

The first edition of the database book was self-published, and it required a lot of work to prepare it for production. Learning how to write and produce a book took a great deal of time but I found it very educational, and I suggest if you have any ambition for writing, you should pursue it.

I learned how to format a book, create my own cover, create a table of contents and appendix, prepare it for binding, and get it to market. I set up an account with Amazon and sold my books there. It was a wonderful learning experience, and I did it all on my own.

It was especially exciting when I connected with Tampa Adult Education to adopt my book for a non-credit course in the database language called SQL and they have been using the book for years.

Shortly after, I was approached by a publisher to publish the book for me. Kendall Hunt Publishing Company contracted the publishing rights to the book, saving me time from managing the promotion and distribution of the book. They also came out with an eBook version that they sell on their website as well as Amazon and Barnes and Noble.

Authoring a book is just another example of starting a business and seeing it through to success. I don't generate significant money from the book, but the rewards of completing a project like that and having people purchase and learn from it is an incredible joy for me, not to mention confidence booster.

If you like to write, I hope you consider writing a book, even a children's book. It's a wonderful learning experience and will educate you about the book writing business as well as provide opportunity to learn more about your capabilities.

Part-Time Entrepreneurship

Deciding to quit a full-time job to start a business has a lot of risks associated with it. Afterall, with a job you have steady income, health insurance, vacation days, sick time, and paid holidays. Running your own full-time business means you will need to be concerned about whether you can afford to take time off, health insurance, and the ability to generate enough income to pay the bills. So, rather than risk everything you have accomplished, think about starting a part-time business and determine its potential for growth before quitting a secure full-time job.

Recently, I had a conversation with a young chiropractor who worked for a physical therapy organization. His goals are to start his own chiropractor practice and become successful enough to be able to support his family. He said he needed to save more money before taking on that risk.

I suggested he try starting a part-time practice first, before giving up a full-time job with a steady income and health benefits for the family. For example, there are many people who would like services at night and weekends so he could build up a clientele using that strategy without giving up his steady cash flow.

Starting off with a part-time business will help you decide how much time, money, and resources you want to put into the business and determine whether you want to take the business full-time or not. You may decide part-time is best with the added security of your full-time job. Many people, including myself, have done this. Some ideas for part-time businesses are as follows:

1. **Landscaping** - Many people have started part-time landscaping businesses and became successful enough to do it full-time. You will need a truck capable of towing lawn equipment and storage space.

This type of business includes start-up costs for equipment so be prepared for that if you choose to do it.

2. **Painting** - I used to paint on my own while in college. My business was word of mouth and each summer I had enough customers to last the summer. Painting takes patience as it can be very messy. Startup costs are small, and you can choose to paint indoors, outdoors, or both. All you need is a ladder, paint brushes, drop cloths and you are good to go.

3. **House Cleaning** - Many people are taking up house cleaning for extra income. Some even do it full-time. Startup costs are relatively small. A vacuum cleaner and cleaning supplies will be enough to get you started.

4. **Tutor** - There is a need for all forms of tutoring in math, writing, computer programing, and SAT exams. I used to hire someone to tutor me with calculus while in college. Likewise, I was paid to tutor others with computer programming. Now that we have video learning you can tutor from home and reach a wider audience.

5. **Social Media Manager** - If you have social media skills, you can help companies with their social

media content and marketing. Social media managers help their clients develop strategies to increase followers by promoting content on various social media platforms.

6. **Wedding Photography** - Many people have taken up photography as a hobby and learned to monetize it with formal events such as weddings. You will need advanced photography skills, a professional camera, and software to edit photos accordingly.

7. **Personal Trainer** - People who have a big interest in fitness can share their knowledge in nutrition and exercise to help others. You should take a certification course before starting to have proper credentials and sell yourself.

8. **Virtual Assistant** - Many small businesses need people with computer skills to provide administrative services such as scheduling, project management, spreadsheet management, and workflows. It's a wonderful stay at home type of business so you can still manage the household while working.

9. **Dog Walker** - Dog walkers are becoming increasingly popular. If you like dogs, it's a fun business. It's best if you can establish yourself in gated

communities so that you can avoid long distance driving to customers.

I know of a woman who was a real estate agent selling homes in a gated community full-time. People who bought from her started asking her if she would walk her dogs. She started part-time and then became so busy she quit real estate and became a full-time dog walker instead.

10. **Mobile Car Washing and Detailing** - This is a low-cost entry business which you can easily do on weekends. You will need to have good car washing supplies, but the water will come from the homeowner.

You would want to try to build up a clientele for repeat business. Also, word of mouth by your customers will go a long way in generating more business.

Famous Successful Entrepreneurs

Many famous entrepreneurs started off with small ideas that bloomed into huge successes. Below I have listed a few you may be familiar with.

1. **Debbi Fields** - Mrs. Fields cookies came from the passion Debbi Fields had for making cookies and making something of herself on her own terms. She

started making cookies at age thirteen and continued into adulthood. She received many compliments on her cookies but when she asked her husband's business acquaintances and friends about starting a cookie business, they all discouraged her.

Debbi decided to pursue her dream anyway and took out a business loan. She opened her first store at the age of twenty and on her first day she didn't have any sales after three hours. She was frustrated but believed in her cookies and herself, so she took to the streets to give out samples. That idea worked as customers came in to purchase cookies after that and that led her to use the strategy of providing samples continuously at her stores.

Debbi eventually grew the company to a huge success resulting in several stores in malls nationwide. In the 1990s Debbi sold the company to an investment firm for one hundred million dollars.

2. **Martha Stewart** - Martha Stewart started her career as a model and followed that with becoming a successful stockbroker. After she left the brokerage firm in 1973, she dedicated her time to renovating a farmhouse in Connecticut as well as pursue her passion for cooking. In 1976 she started a catering business that she ran from home. Over a ten-year period she was able to generate an income of over one million dollars.

Among Martha's clients were publishers. She leveraged those connections to produce a book deal on cooking. She followed that with more books on domestic matters such as home restoration, gardening, weddings, and Christmas. In 1990 Martha started her own magazine called *Martha Stewart Living* and followed that with a television show in 1993 with the same name.

Martha Stewart followed her passion for gardening, cooking, and homemaking to become a household name and multi-millionaire.

3. **Mark Cuban** - Mark Cuban found the spirit for entrepreneurship at age twelve when he started selling garbage bags door to door to earn money to buy a pair of shoes that he was fond of. At the age of sixteen he saw that a local newspaper was on strike so he ordered newspapers from another city and sold them in his area until the strike ended. In college he offered dancing lessons on campus for twenty-five dollars an hour. Later he bought a bar with his friends and turned it into one of the most popular college hangouts in town.

    After college Mark got a job as a computer software salesman but was fired within a year. So, he started a business called Micro Solutions to compete with his former employer called Micro Solutions and eventually sold it for six million dollars. In

1995 Mark invested ten thousand dollars in a company called AudioNet that offered streaming services for sporting events. He renamed the company Broadcast.com and managed it to success, eventually selling the business for 5.7 billion dollars to Yahoo in 1998.

Mark has been an entrepreneur all his working life. His vision and ambition have led him to start and build many successful businesses. He is a self-made billionaire who is owner of the Dallas Mavericks and regular investor on *Shark Tank*.

4. **Barbara Corcoran** - Barbara Corcoran grew up poor in a two-bedroom apartment with her mother and nine siblings. In high school she was a very poor student because of her challenges with dyslexia. But she didn't let her poor grades get in the way of her ambition and creativity.

    At age twenty-three, she quit her job working as a waitress to become a receptionist at a real estate company. Learning how the real estate business worked, Barbara borrowed one thousand dollars from her boyfriend to start a real estate firm. She asked her boss at the real estate company if she could try renting one of his apartments out and he agreed. She compared the one-bedroom apartment to other one-bedroom apartments and found they were similar in structure and price. She got creative and asked her boss to build a wall as a divider so that she could sell it as a one-bedroom and den. The result was several phone calls of interest and a contract to rent.

Since that first success, Barbara used her ambition and creativity to create her own real estate business called the Corcoran Group, resulting in a multi-million-dollar company.

5. **Daymond John** - Daymond John grew up in Queens, New York, and started working at the age of six selling pencils and shoveling snow. When he turned ten, he became an electrician apprentice and wired PX cable in abandoned buildings in the Bronx.

When Daymond was in his teenage years he was working as a waiter at Red Lobster. Around this time, he was introduced to hip-hop music and was an immediate fan. He and his friends started wearing the same clothes as the hip-hop artists which inspired him to come up with the idea of his own clothing line. He called the company FUBU (For Us By Us).

Daymond learned how to sew from his mother and used her house to grow the business. He first created wool hats and sold them in the streets making eight hundred dollars a day. Then he moved on to screen-printed T-shirts. While working at growing his business, Daymond continued to work at Red Lobster to help pay the bills.

Daymond needed startup capital, so his mother mortgaged the house to recruit and pay friends to help with sewing. He eventually convinced rap stars to wear his clothing in videos. In 1994 Daymond received three hundred thousand dollars in orders and an offer to participate in Macy's Las Vegas fashion trade show.

FUBU has gone on to become a six-billion-dollar business because of hard work, vision, and the determination of Daymond John.

6. **Two Men and a Truck** - This company started out in the early 1980s with two high school brothers, Brig and John Sorber, who wanted to make extra money by moving people in the with an old pickup truck they had. Their mother, Mary Ellen Sheets, came up with the logo below and advertised the business in a local newspaper.

After her sons went to college in 1985, Mary continued with the business by purchasing a fourteen-foot truck for three-hundred-fifty dollars and hiring two movers. In 1989 it was suggested she franchise the business. The company now has over three thousand trucks nation-wide.

7. **College Hunks Hauling Junk & Moving** - In 2003 Oscar Soliman was a twenty-one-year-old college student who saw an opportunity to make money during summer break. His mother owned a furniture store and often customers asked if they could haul the old furniture away during deliveries. This prompted Oscar to borrow his mother's cargo van and partner with his friend, Nick Friedman, to haul junk away. They came up with the name "College Hunks Hauling Junk."

Omar created flyers and put them around the neighborhood. Within twenty-four hours they got phone calls and started making money. Their first summer with the new business generated over eight thousand dollars.

After graduating both Omar and Nick started office jobs. But they realized it was boring work and decided to make their business their full-time occupation. College Hunks Hauling Junk is now worth an estimated two-hundred-fifty million dollars.

Characteristics of Successful Entrepreneurs

Even though successful entrepreneurs come from various backgrounds and upbringings they tend to share some basic characteristics that lead to their successes.

1. **Passion** - People who have great passion for their interests find joy in the work involved in pursuing them. Passion is what motivates entrepreneurs past the trials and tribulations towards their goals.

   I recall reading a story about Robert Mondavi, a highly successful wine maker out of Napa Valley. Before going off on his own he was involved in the wine-making business with his family called CK Mondavi. In 1965 Robert got into a family feud which led to the family buying him out of the business. At the age of fifty-wto Robert decided to start his own winery. When asked why he wanted to continue working since he was already worth millions, he simply said, "It is my passion." Robert went on to become highly successful with the Robert Mondavi Winery using his passion and creativity to promote Napa Valley as a tourist destination producing world class wines.

2. **Discipline** - Entrepreneurs tend to be disciplined both in their personal and working lives. They have structure in their lives and balance many activities to get things done on time and in a professional manner. I personally have been very disciplined in my studies, work, exercise, and eating habits throughout the years. This has led to a healthy and energetic lifestyle allowing me to participate in many interests, both work related and pleasure.

3. **Drive to Succeed** - Entrepreneurs stand out from others because they have a strong desire to succeed and reach their goals. They enjoy the challenges, so it's not just work for them. They don't let failures dissuade them. They are resilient and use failures as learning lessons along the way to success.

4. **Visionary** - Entrepreneurs tend to be visionaries who enjoy coming up with ideas to create products and services. They are inquisitive and enjoy using their minds in creative ways.

5. **Disconnecting** - Entrepreneurs have difficulty putting their business aside to enjoy their personal lives. They tend to check emails, text, and think about business activities even during vacations. This is a trait anybody who is an entrepreneur or wants to be one needs to keep in mind. While it's good to succeed in business, it is also important to succeed in our personal lives as well, so balance is necessary.

6. **Boredom** - Entrepreneurs are easily bored. They have difficulty doing the same task repeatedly as one might on a job. Once they complete a project successfully, they are ready for their next one. Some may say they should relax and enjoy the rewards, but that doesn't give them pleasure—challenge does. Even if they sell their business and become millionaires, they will look for another venture.

    Remember, your family is important too. While you may have the desire to look for new projects, think of the happiness of your family as your most important project. For example, I have many projects going on, but nothing makes me happier than getting my family together for big gatherings.

7. **Taking Risks** - Entrepreneurs take risks and take a chance of losing. But entrepreneurs are resilient and will bounce back. They have the drive and creativity to come up with other ideas to make an income.

Certainly, working for a company is secure, but it's boring to an entrepreneur. As an entrepreneur you can explore your creativity and use your desire to reach your goals as opposed to someone else's.

8. **Adaptable** - To continue to succeed in business, entrepreneurs need to be adaptable to change in society. For example, during the Covid pandemic, many restaurants suffered and went out of business. Others changed their business model to take-out orders and made enough to survive until the pandemic was over.

   Another example is how the schools survived during the pandemic. Thankfully technology was available to allow video training. This resulted in many new schools forming that strictly teach online as opposed to a classroom.

9. **Self-Branding** - Entrepreneurs do not separate themselves from the business. They represent the business just as the business represents them. It is part of their identity.

10. **Hard Working** - Without a doubt, successful entrepreneurs work very hard and often work many hours beyond the typical forty-hour work week. They are driven to succeed so they don't view the work the same as they would working for a company they

don't own. As mentioned earlier, a company they own is part of their identity, so they are very determined to do whatever it takes to succeed.

Owning your own business is a very rewarding experience. Besides the income potential, you will learn more about yourself as you explore ideas and see them through to fruition. You will need to develop business strategies to gain customers, manage expenses, and increase profits. You may experience setbacks, failures, and struggles but you should learn to be resilient. Motivate yourself with lessons learned and move on to your next try at entrepreneurship. It's a very empowering experience that will improve your self-esteem and confidence to serve you a lifetime.

Chapter 7

Career
Stagnation

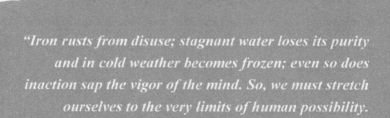

*"Iron rusts from disuse; stagnant water loses its purity
and in cold weather becomes frozen; even so does
inaction sap the vigor of the mind. So, we must stretch
ourselves to the very limits of human possibility.
Anything less is a sin against both God and man."*

—LEONARDO DA VINCI

There may be times when you find your career growth has been stunted at a company. Often people blame the company for lack of upward mobility. While the company may not be helping our careers, we are still in charge of ourselves, and it is up to us to do something about it.

It's important to recognize and understand why your career has stopped growing and then act to do something about it. This chapter will discuss possible causes for career stagnation and explain some strategies to overcome it.

Company Rejection

I had the good fortune of talking to someone who taught me that many times a job candidate from outside the company will have a better chance of being selected for a position over candidates inside the company. He explained that this is due to the hiring team being aware of all aspects of an internal candidate—strengths, weaknesses, and personality. Whereas outside candidates are new, so their true personalities and weaknesses are not yet known. Certainly, during the interview process the candidates will be on their best and most enthusiastic behavior. Discussions will be primarily on accomplishments and strengths of the candidates. Any discussion on weaknesses that may affect employment will, of course, be avoided.

When we meet new people, it is natural to have positive thoughts about them as we have little or no reason to think otherwise. As we get to know them better, we will find whether the friendship chemistry is a match and understand better how close the individual will be in our lives. Some new relationships will develop into strong friendships while others will remain acquaintances because the chemistry is lacking for a stronger relationship. The same happens in the workplace. As we get to know our co-workers, we better understand how they fit in with the organization, team, and culture. Over time we learn the strengths new employees bring to the team and whether they fit in culturally.

As an example, I will share a workplace situation where an internal candidate was shunned for a full-time faculty position at my college. I was working as a full-time professor when I volunteered to join the hiring committee for a full-time math professor position. There were four of us on the hiring committee altogether and we accepted applications from external and internal candidates. The one internal candidate that applied had worked for the college as an adjunct math professor for a couple of years. I will address her as Mary to avoid using her real name to protect her privacy.

I admired Mary a great deal. While I didn't teach the same courses as Mary, as I was a computer science professor and she taught math, my office was in the same vicinity as her desk so I got to converse with her quite often. I found her to be charming and someone who deeply cared about her students. She was a very pleasant individual with what seemed to be a permanent smile. The students liked her very much. It was obvious that she cared for them and always made herself available to help outside the classroom.

The hiring committee had interviewed five people from outside the college as well as Mary, our internal adjunct candidate. After interviewing all the candidates, the committee had to choose three candidates to move forward to the next round of interviews. We began conversations about the strengths of all the candidates and we shared our opinions and made our choices. I was the only one who thought Mary should move forward to the next round. The others admired Mary but reflected on minor weaknesses they were aware of because of her history with the college. I honestly cannot recall specifically what they didn't like about Mary, but I remember it was minor, and they would not know anything about it if Mary was an external candidate.

I explained to the committee that, "Mary is at a disadvantage by being an internal candidate because we know everything about her, including possible weaknesses. For example, we know how her personality fits into our culture, and we have access to her dean and student evaluations. On the contrary, we only know the strengths of the external candidates based on their resumes and what they tell us about themselves at the interviews. We are not using the same factors in judging the external candidates as we are Mary. We all like Mary, and agree she is a capable teacher, or we wouldn't keep her as an adjunct. Yet, the committee has brought up minor weaknesses that we know about only because she teaches here."

The committee responded by saying, "That's not true." I explained further that, "It is very true as I heard no one discuss the background and history of the other candidates and that's simply because we don't know anything about them other than what they are telling us and what is on their resumes. We are unable to talk about student and dean evaluations regarding the other candidates like we can with Mary. I find, certainly, Mary is at a disadvantage."

It did not matter how I explained it and how much I fought for Mary, she was not selected to continue to move forward to the next phase of the hiring process.

This had to be a significant blow to Mary's confidence and self-esteem. I felt bad and let her know I was cheering for her because I believed in her and I was confident in her abilities as a teacher. I advised her not to give up and seek out other colleges for full-time employment. I offered myself as a referral as well.

What happened to Mary is something that you should be aware of because it can happen to you. Unfortunately, this is part of working life. If this happens to you, don't take it personally and avoid being emotional about it. There is no benefit to it. Instead, use it as a hint that it's time to move on to the next step in life and look for better opportunities to grow your career.

Any time you feel your true potential isn't being recognized, prepare yourself to move on. But keep your job until you land another one and never show disenchanted emotions. It's a small world and you never know when you will meet former co-workers and managers again on your professional path to success.

▓ Smaller Companies

Some people enjoy working at small companies that don't have plans for growth. It feels safe and secure to them, and it is usually more personable. There is an opportunity to develop good relationships because there is a feeling of community. Some people also enjoy being a "big fish in a small pond." In other words, they are very important to the operations of the small company and are involved in many functionalities of the company. On the contrary, employees at large companies tend to work in silos and usually only learn their part of the operation unless they take it upon themselves to move into other positions.

Smaller companies tend to be good training ground for people new to the workforce because they expose the employee to various positions outside their normal job responsibilities. Quite often, small companies will ask employees to overlap job functions. It can be a rewarding experience to be involved in so many job functions.

As good as the learning experience is at small companies, unless it's a growing company there is less upward mobility because of the limited number of positions available. If you are interested in being a manager, for example, you may have to wait until the current one leaves. This will limit your salary potential and career growth.

If you are interested in learning new business practices or software technologies that are popular in the industry, small companies may leave you with antiquated skills because they usually aren't so quick to adapt to the latest industry standards. I worked for a small organization once that was using computer resources from a company going out of business. Despite the great people I worked with, I decided to leave to learn new skills and stay current with technology.

If you find yourself at a small company and desire career and salary growth and there is no growth with the company itself, you will have to consider leaving for another company that can provide the growth path you seek. Before doing so, you will need to learn what the industry is looking for in terms of skills and, if necessary, take action to train yourself. Remember, job security is dependent on your employability and your employability is dependent on your staying current with skill sets.

There are many startup companies that start off small but have desire to grow into larger companies. Unlike small companies that have been around for a while and have little desire to grow, startup companies are fast-moving with changes occurring frequently so you would be exposed to a lot of different learning opportunities. These types of companies can provide ample career growth and the experience you can get will serve you well for employment at other companies.

▨ **Too Good to Promote**

When I was in college I was working at a supermarket and every Saturday I had to be there at seven a.m. to stock the shelves. Inside the back room of the supermarket there were three people who started at five a.m. One person was responsible for taking the packages that were delivered in large dolly trucks, placing them on the conveyor belt, and cutting the top lid open. The second person was responsible for pricing the opened package. The third person, I will call him Joe, was responsible for placing each box on to smaller dolly trucks to wheel out to specific aisles by the shelf stockers like me. Joe had the hardest job of all. He had to be quick and place the right products on the right dolly trucks associated with each aisle in the store. At times there weren't enough dolly trucks, so the packages had to be taken off the conveyor belt and placed on the floor until more dolly trucks were available. So, not only did Joe have to continue moving packages off the conveyor belt onto dolly trucks, but he had to move the boxes off the floor that he couldn't put on dolly trucks earlier. It was the hardest job and the least rewarding. It also didn't pay any better than the stocker positions. I was glad I didn't have to do it.

One month, Joe was out for a few weeks due to illness, so they were assigning the stockers at random to do the job that Joe did. After a few weeks it was my turn, so I got up early, punched in at five a.m. and started unloading the packages from the conveyor belt and placed them onto the appropriate dolly trucks for the stockers. The following Saturday they had me do it again. Then the Saturday after that as well. When Joe came back from his illness the management had him stock shelves and assigned me his previous job even though he was perfectly capable of doing it. I didn't like coming in at five a.m. so I asked if I could go back to stocking shelves starting at seven a.m. Management answered, "No." I asked why and they said, "Because you're the fastest. No one else is as fast as you are unloading the packages from the conveyor belt, so this is your new job." I learned a big lesson that day. Not only was I not rewarded for doing good work, but I was also now stuck with a job I disliked because I was better at it than anybody else.

This type of management mindset followed me during my professional career as well. Being a successful software developer, I had skills that were hard to find and in big demand. Often, I would continue to develop applications with good but older technology that provided no increased skill sets for me, so I asked to be put on new projects that were using updated technology. I was often denied because my skill set was needed with the older technology and no one else knew how to do it.

There was a time I wanted to make a change in my career to a less technical role. I saw an opportunity I was perfectly capable of doing in my department for a business analyst role. Being a software developer, I knew in detail how the business functioned because I had to code applications for it. When I asked my manager if I could be considered for the role she said, "No, your skills are too valuable in the application development area, and you are hard to replace." So, even though my manager respected me and regarded me as being important to her department, she refused to reward me by allowing me to grow. If I stayed in her department, my professional growth would be stunted. I understood my manager's position, she had responsibilities to fulfill, but I had my goals to pursue. It was now up to me to take action for my growth. Within a year I left the department and moved on to another role with no grudges. It was a very pleasant parting of ways.

If you are interested in growing your career and feel you are stunted in your current situation, take the initiative to plan your next move. Learn the types of skills companies are hiring for, if necessary update your skill set, polish your resume, and apply for new positions. Don't leave your current position angry. Instead understand that everyone has their own objectives so focus on yours and pursue your growth. Always stay professional and never resign with a grudge.

▓ Boredom

After learning a job and doing it for some time without new challenges, you might get bored. Some people are comfortable with this but it's not a mindset for growth or steady employment.

One of the dangers of boredom is that you don't get to exercise your mind. When your mind is not challenged it becomes less responsive and you lose cognitive ability much like you lose physical ability when not exercising. So, you may not be as sharp as you need to be when interviewing for another position.

Another danger with a boring job is the loss of skills. A job is never guaranteed so you need to make sure you are employable for other opportunities. Keep learning skills that the industry needs.

If you find yourself bored, look around for opportunities where you might be able to help in your department. As a software developer I have skills that allow me to automate processes, so I look for those opportunities. But if you find there are not any opportunities to work on, try asking your manager for more responsibilities. The other option is to move on to a more challenging role.

Lack of Work

Be very careful when you find there isn't enough work to keep you busy. Not only does this cause boredom, but you will put yourself in danger of being laid off.

I had a friend who was hired at a new job for a computer networking position. She was very excited, and I was very happy for her. After a couple of weeks at the job I met up with her and asked her about the job. She said, "All I've been doing is attending meetings. I really haven't been given any work yet." A few more weeks went by, and I got the same response. She had not received any assignments or responsibilities. This is a major red flag, and you need to watch out for this because it can lead to losing your job. Eventually, my friend did lose her job and I knew it was going to happen after the second time she told me she had nothing to do.

Quite often departments may find there is money in the budget to hire people, so managers might add to their staff without giving much thought to the specifics of the job. They may have a rough idea on how the new position could be of help to the department, but they don't always provide a path for the new employee to stay busy and succeed. Or, they simply don't have the time to give it thought. I had this happen to me once. Luckily, I am resourceful with my software skills so I used my skills to automate manual processes and added value that way. For example, I saw a process that was taking fifteen hours a week to perform. I asked my manager if I could use my skill set to improve on the process. She agreed and I went to work. That process no longer takes human intervention. It runs on its own.

I wasn't asked to automate the process, but like I was mentioning earlier, look around and see how you can add value. Once my manager saw how I could be useful, she had me automate several other processes and I began to feel comfortable that I wouldn't lose my job. Also, it was a boost to my self-esteem.

If you find yourself in a position with no real responsibilities or assignments, once again, look around and see how you might be able to do something to add value. If you really can't find anything, then you will need to meet with your manager to discuss opportunities. Managers are busy so they may be having a difficult time planning an assignment or project for you to work on. Try not to think they are ignoring you. When I couldn't find anything else to do, I found time on their calendar to meet with them to discuss assignments. Usually that will work. But if it doesn't, prepare to look for another job. Remember, your employment is dependent on your employability so if you don't have work to do you are not improving your skill set.

Career Growth

There are a couple of approaches to grow your career, vertically and horizontally. Vertically follows the career ladder approach and results in higher positions, responsibilities, and salary. The horizontal approach is called the career lattice and is associated with moving to roles at the same level in an organization but with different responsibilities.

- **Career Ladder** - The career ladder path is the traditional growth path to work your way up the organization structure. It's vertical growth and usually encompasses a specialized skill set. People who choose this path are looking for higher titles in a specific area. For example, a career in accounting has positions for vertical growth such as staff accountant, senior accountant, accounting supervisor, accounting manager, and controller.

- **Career Lattice** - A lattice career path translates to horizontal growth. So instead of working towards the next higher position, you change roles to learn new skills and not necessarily a higher pay level, although you can climb the ladder upward this way too. Changing roles will help you avoid boredom and expose you to many facets of the business. You will work with a variety of departments and teams exposing you to strong networking opportunities and increasing your worth to the organization. In addition, you will gain a broad skill set resulting in many employment opportunities for your future.

Keep Your Skills Updated

To ensure I had the skills that were in demand I jumped around quite a bit in my career to learn new skills. Sometimes I took a pay cut to gain experience in new technology that would provide opportunities in the future. I always thought strategically for the long term as opposed to the short term.

So, sacrificing pay for long term goals was worth it to me. I looked at it as being paid to learn new skills.

After almost forty years, I have never been laid off. I avoided layoffs by understanding what skills were needed in the industry and then took time to learn them. I never allowed my skills to diminish. Keep this in mind when thinking about your career longevity.

Returning to school is a good idea to enhance your skills or work towards a second career. I returned to college to obtain a master's degree in Computer Information Technology at the age of forty-two so that I could teach as a college professor. But the degree and teaching led me to other paths of growth professionally and personally. I became better at public speaking and project planning which helped me in the corporate world. During my master's studies I had to perform a lot of research and write several papers leading to improved writing skills. So, don't think of returning to school as a chore. Instead, embrace it and get the most you can out of it.

If you want to stay in demand for employment and get more out of your career and personal life, then "don't sit the bench." Take on new challenges to keep growing. Doing so will make you more valuable to employers and, most importantly, strengthen your self-esteem.

Chapter 8

Social Capital

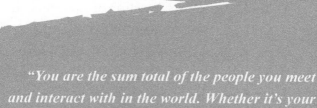

"You are the sum total of the people you meet
and interact with in the world. Whether it's your
family, peers, or co-workers, the opportunities
you have and the things that you learn all come
through doors that other people open for you."

—TANNER COLBY

Your social environment is made up of your family, friends, peers at work, school, and any other people you socialize with in your life. The value you receive from your social interactions makes up your social capital. The relationships you develop will greatly impact your professional and personal life.

Building your social capital is as important as building your skill sets. The stronger your social capital the more opportunities you will have for career advancement. Become cognizant of who you have relationships with, as it will have great influence on your future. Building a network of underachievers can take you in the opposite direction of success.

▦ Types of Social Capital

Let's begin by describing the types of social capital we experience in our lives. I've outlined three below.

1. **Bonding** - We have all had experiences bonding with family and friends. Bonding social capital involves close relationships attributed to shared characteristics among people such as the same social economic group, age, sports, and clubs. Certainly, if you play sports, you have a strong bond among your teammates and support one another.

    Recently, four wrestling students from Northwest College in Powell, Wyoming, were on an expedition to find antlers in Shoshone National Forest. Two of them, Brayden Lowry and Kendell Cummings, separated from the other two and found themselves in the company of a grizzly bear. The bear attacked and knocked down Lowry. Cummings went to his friend's rescue and started punching the bear but then the bear turned and started to attack him.

Cummings was fighting the bear and protecting his face and neck from bites by the bear when it stopped and started to walk away. He then rose to find Lowry, but then the bear attacked again. Once again, the bear walked away from that attack as well.

Cummings was hurt very badly so Lowry ran up the mountain to be able to call 911. He was able to find his other teammates and they all helped Cummings down the mountain for medical attention. Luckily, the wounds were not life threatening and both Lowry and Cummings were expected to make full recoveries after having gone through multiple surgeries.

The story of the college wrestlers is a good example of bonding. They had tight bonds as teammates before the bear attack, but now that they experienced such a traumatic event, their bond grew even stronger.

Think about your close relationships today and the degree of bonding you have with them. Certainly, these relationships should be cherished because they mean so much our personal lives.

2. **Bridging** - Your friend introducing you to his/her friend is an example of bridging social capital. While these relationships are not as strong as bonding, they are important to expanding your network for opportunities. You may not share the same characteristics in a bridging relationship but bridging usually consists of people from the same social economic background. These friendships expose you to a diverse population leading to increased understanding of society.

Many times I have been called the nucleus of gatherings among my friends because I have brought many who are in different social circles together at parties or simple dinners. This is a perfect example of bridging. Some of these relationships ended up with friends joining other social circles. It's a wonderful way to find new friends as well as build your social capital.

I remember a time when I was introduced to someone who worked in human resources, and he offered to help me find a position at his company. I did not know him before that first day of introduction but bridging in this way helped me find a job.

3. **Linking** - Linking social capital occurs in relationships with different social economic backgrounds. For example, a CEO of a company and the day-to-day staff. The CEO can benefit by his relationship with staff by understanding the work among staff for possible improvements. Staff can benefit with advice for growth from the CEO.

I remember a time when my company put on a charity event that involved meeting the CEOs of the company to raise money for people in need. I contributed and got to meet one of the CEOs for lunch. I found the conversation fascinating. He offered advice on my career path, and he enjoyed learning the type of work I was doing for the company and my goals.

Personal Examples of Social Capital

If we feel stunted in our growth both professionally and personally, it may be time to increase your social capital. We don't need to alienate existing friends, but if you want to grow you may need develop new relationships with people who share the same interests and goals that you have.

I have friends that work in various jobs—construction, trades, business owners, corporate professionals, and some retired from the workforce. I have moved on to different paths in life that I am unable to share with some long-time friends. But they still are part of my community. I continue to enhance my social capital with new people who share my new interests and growth and develop new relationships. But my older friends are still a big part of my social circle and I value their relationships.

After graduating high school, I didn't attend college right away. Instead, I took a full-time job at a paint store and hung out with the same group of people had I hung out with in high school who also didn't go to college. Together we talked about who was unemployed, our jobs, music, and sports. None of us seemed to like our jobs, but we weren't doing anything about it. It was a very unproductive time in my life. I felt strange as I wasn't in school anymore, and I didn't feel like I was growing. I was completely lost and unsure of what to do.

After about a year I decided to attend a community college in my state and almost immediately felt a positive change. I now had a goal to achieve, an associate degree in Management Information Systems. While enrolling in college was a big positive change for me, equally as positive was making new friends with people who also had similar goals. Socializing in this new circle changed my way of thinking. I didn't stop seeing my old friends, but I was spending less time with them because enhancing my social capital put new ideas in my mind and I had different interests and a new perspective on life. My mind was on schoolwork, working towards my degree, and professional employment, all topics I could discuss with my new friends but not my older friends.

Many of my new friends had plans to transfer to a university after they received their associate degree and that inspired me to do the same. Once at the university I met more people who shared their goals and their objectives in reaching them. This enhanced my thinking for my path towards my goals. With my new friends I started thinking about opportunities I had not considered.

I also met a young dynamic woman who I shared common interests with, and we started dating. When I think back at my days before college, I could not have met such a wonderful woman if I had not enhanced my social circle by going to college. My life is so much more fulfilling because of the exposure I have had meeting so many different people.

The Roseto Effect

It's important to understand how social capital is attributed to good health, especially bonding social capital. The perfect example of this is the study of a small town in Pennsylvania called Roseto that served an Italian population who immigrated from Italy starting in 1887 and continuing into the 1960s. They were forced to build a community amongst themselves because they were shunned by the neighboring towns. They lived this way for decades and the community became a haven for them.

During the 1950s and early 1960s two doctors were intrigued by the low rate of heart disease amongst the people of Roseto compared to the surrounding population. The food of the Roseto people, although good tasting, wasn't any healthier than the rest of the population. They ate sausage, cheese, salami, pepperoni, and egg, all of which contribute to heart disease.

The study looked at other Italians that came from the same area in Italy as the Roseto citizens to determine if it was genetic. They found, unlike the people of Roseto, that they were not as healthy. So, they ruled out genetics as the reason for low rates of heart disease in Roseto.

The study also looked at the environment and the possibility of the water being a factor. But since the water being used by the Roseto community was also serving surrounding communities that was ruled out too.

After researching all possibilities for low heart disease levels, the study concluded that it was the supportive behavior of the Roseto community as the reason for better heart health. Stress was low due to the strong and close relationships of the community. There were three or for generations living in the same home so it was common to see grandparents living in the same homes as grandchildren. They had many celebrations throughout the community including religious events. Everyone in the community was very supportive so no one ever felt alone.

Later in the mid-1960s, the children of Roseto started to adapt to the American lifestyle such as long work hours, bagged lunches, processed foods, and isolation that resulted in an increase in heart problems as well as other health issues.

While bridging and linking social capital provide op-portunities to grow our lives with access to people willing to share information and successes, bonding is important to our mental and physical wellbeing. The Roseto study clearly demonstrates the importance of building a close community with family and friends.

Chapter 9

Emotional
Intelligence

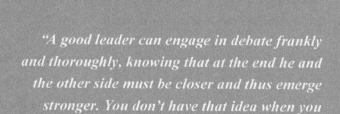

*"A good leader can engage in debate frankly
and thoroughly, knowing that at the end he and
the other side must be closer and thus emerge
stronger. You don't have that idea when you
are arrogant, superficial, and uninformed."*

—NELSON MANDELA

We all have experienced a range of positive and negative emotions. For example, we experience joy when receiving a gift or a good grade on an exam. Negative emotions include feeling angry about something such as your car being vandalized or feeling depressed over losing a game. This is common to human nature. However, to help ensure our relationships stay strong and secure, it is important to understand and control our emotions, especially when conflict occurs. Emotional intelligence involves the ability to recognize and manage our own emotions as well as being empathetic to other people's emotions to help us foster positive relationships in our lives.

🐜 Controlling Anger

We need to learn to become self-aware of our emotions to act in a positive manner. If you are stressed or angry, your emotions may control you rather than you controlling them. Too often, in times of conflict, the wrong words are expressed that can cause damage to relationships, sometimes irreparable damage. Below I have included a story that expresses the harm that can come from uncontrolled anger.

"There once was a little boy who had a very bad temper. His father decided to hand him a bag of nails and said that every time the boy lost his temper, he had to hammer a nail into the fence.

On the first day, the boy hammered thirty-seven nails into that fence.

The boy gradually began to control his temper over the next few weeks, and the number of nails he was hammering into the fence slowly decreased. He discovered it was easier to control his temper than to hammer those nails into the fence.

Finally, the day came when the boy didn't lose his temper at all. He told his father the news and the father suggested that the boy should now pull out a nail every day he kept his temper under control.

The days passed and the young boy was finally able to tell his father that all the nails were gone. The father took his son by the hand and led him to the fence.

'You have done well, my son, but look at the holes in the fence. The fence will never be the same. When you say things in anger, they leave a scar just like this one. You can put a knife in a man and draw it out. It won't matter how many times you say I'm sorry, the wound is still there.'

Story by ThoughtCatalog.com

Words alone can cause a lifetime of damage to relationships, so it is important to be aware of your anger and to learn to control it. It's not always easy and it may take practice, but if you are willing to do the work it's possible. Below are some suggestions for controlling anger.

- **Abdominal Breathing** - A wonderful relaxing technique is to breathe from your diaphragm and not your chest. Feel your stomach fill with air and let it out slowly, even watching it in your mind. This will naturally help you relax while slowing your heartbeat and lowering blood pressure.

- **Thoughts of Calmness** - Think of something that calms you. For me, I love the feel of the breeze on a beach and hearing the ocean waves, so I use that scene to calm me down. Abdominal breathing and relaxing thoughts will help you destress quickly.

    Recently, I went for a physical checkup and my blood pressure was a bit high, so the doctor asked me to sit for a few minutes, breathe, and think about something relaxing. I thought about pets and how warm and loving they are. When the doctor returned to check my blood pressure again, it was reduced by twenty points.

- **Take a Walk** - If you are in conflict and don't quite know how to respond and are in danger of saying the wrong thing, excuse yourself and take a walk. Walks are wonderful ways to release energy and clear the mind to think things out. By taking a walk you will show that you are aware of your emotional state and taking action to relax before responding instead of reacting and causing damage to the relationship.

- **Avoid an Argument** - If it's possible, avoid conflict with those who have made up their minds and are inflexible. We don't need to convince anybody to agree with our point of view if they wish not to. There's a phrase I like, "Pick your battles." If something isn't really that important, there is no need to enter conflict.

The emotionally intelligent mind thinks in terms of defusing conflict rather than contributing to it. Learn to listen to the other person and understand why he/she is upset. Offer empathy for their concerns and remain calm. By remaining calm, we can help others become more relaxed. Once the stress level is down and everyone is more relaxed, there is opportunity for rational discussions to take place.

Understanding Emotions of Others

If we are to become emotionally intelligent, it is important to understand not only how we feel, but how others feel as well. We want to act in ways that support our relationships and not tear them down. We need to be perceptive to understand how others will feel from our actions. The following is a true story to help demonstrate the need for understanding the emotions of others.

A very intelligent young lady, I'll call her Sarah to protect her identity, was a quick learner and retained information from reading and lectures easily. Her roommate, I'll call

Joanne, although intelligent as well, wasn't as quick a leaner and had to study a great deal more than Sarah.

One day Joanne was studying in her dorm room when Sarah walked in. Joanne asked, "Aren't you going to study for the test?" Sarah replied, "No, I'm good, I don't have to." Sarah's response triggered negative emotions with Joanne and resulted in straining their relationship.

Let's take a minute to understand what emotions are involved in this situation. Imagine you are stressed out from studying for hours while your roommate is completely relaxed and very confidently says she doesn't have to study. Might that make you feel several negative emotions such as anger, inferiority, depression, and perhaps jealousy?

Some might say Joanne shouldn't have experienced anything negative by Sarah's answer. Others might say Sarah acted smugly and was insensitive. But let's not worry about who was right or wrong and how each of them acted because that would lead to gossip with no good resolution. Instead, it's far more productive to understand how emotional intelligence understanding and strategies could have been used to prevent the relationship from damage.

How could Sarah and Joanne have avoided straining their relationship? If both learned and practiced emotional intelligence, the relationship could have continued without repercussions. Let's consider Sarah's actions first and determine how she could have acted differently. Practicing emotional intelligence means being perceptive of other's feelings. For Joanne, it must be frustrating to be stressed out and work so hard at her studies while her roommate is completely relaxed. To help Joanne feel better and not feel so alone in her struggles, Sarah could have used a white lie to say that she had studied a lot already and then offer to discuss some of the material with Joanne. Even if it's a white lie, it is best to be empathetic to Joanne's situation and offer encouragement and possibly some help.

How could Joanne have acted? Joanne could have practiced emotional intelligence by being aware of how she was feeling and staying in control rather than letting her emotions control her. It's not easy, but the more we practice controlling our emotions, the more natural and instinctive it will become.

We should do our best in helping others feel good rather than tear them down. Doing so will increase your social capital and build your self-esteem. You will feel good about yourself. Confident, intelligent, and secure people don't need to promote themselves. Instead, they inspire and encourage others to be the same way.

Leadership

Great leaders are those who have a high degree of emotional intelligence. Their ability to be aware of their own emotions as well as their staff's benefits the development of a strong organization. Below are four traits good leaders share to promote a strong and productive staff.

- **Impact on others** - It is important for leaders to stay measured and in control even in times of controversy to promote positive decision making and performance among their staff. The staff is looking to leaders to define the culture of the team and to set examples of how to operate for the benefit of the organization. A leader must understand their behavior will be followed by subordinates, so it is important to stay in control even in the most distressing situations.

- **Empathetic** - When members of staff are going through a difficult time good leaders are those who are able to understand what they are going through as well as have the ability to feel what they are going through. It's important and respectful to let staff know that you have their best interest in mind. A respected employee is a productive employee.

- **Positive atmosphere** - Successful leaders understand the importance of maintaining a positive atmosphere. They do this by creating a culture where employees don't feel threatened, but instead feel secure and supported. Good leaders want to help their employees succeed, not diminish their self-esteem.

- **Self-management** - Leaders who practice emotional intelligence first recognize their emotions and then process them before responding to situations.

Instead of scolding a staff member, for example, they come up with ideas to offer positive feedback for performance improvement.

❀ Electronic Communication

Each day we communicate electronically using text, email, and social media. While electronic communication is convenient, there are dangers to it that we need to be aware of, especially when experiencing negative emotions. Below is a list of suggestions to think about when communicating electronically.

- **Email** - Don't ever send an emotionally negative email. Always stay professional and calm. If you must reply to a stressful email take as much time as you can to get to a calm state and think about your response to defuse the stressful situation. If you think it's possible that an email could be perceived with the wrong intention, send an emoticon with it. I often send a happy face emoticon to show I only have positive interest in mind.

- **Texting** - Sometimes texting can result in a different understanding than we intended. I've been in situations where I sent a text in a joking way, but it was construed as serious. Once again, emoticons help provide the mood and attitude of the text so that the recipient understands the correct intent.

- **Social Media** - When using social media, refrain from any negative content. Anything you put on social media can follow you anywhere and impact employment opportunities as well as your personal life. When using social media always remain positive and do not react. Think before posting.

Emotional Intelligence Principles

To become emotionally intelligent, you should understand the following basic principles:

- **Self-awareness** - Take the time to analyze your emotions and understand how they make you react. Doing so can help you change your behavior for more positive outcomes as well as help you avoid situations that are nonproductive. Before responding think about your emotions and how you can project a positive outcome.

- **Others' emotions** - Become aware of the emotions of others to keep relationships strong. Use empathy to help feel what others are feeling and become helpful. Learn to defuse difficult situations so that they don't result in broken relationships.

- **Self-control** - Learn to be in control of your emotions. There will be situations that make you angry, but rather than reacting, learn to act after giving it rational thought to achieve the best outcomes. Nelson Mandela said, "If you want to make peace with your enemy, you have to work with your enemy. Then he becomes your partner."

Learning to become emotionally intelligent will help you gain great strides in your professional and personal life. Using these principles will help you build strong healthy relationships and do wonders for developing your social capital.

Chapter 10

Mentorship

"The delicate balance of mentoring someone is not creating them in your own image but giving them the opportunity to create themselves."

—STEVEN SPIELBERG

A good mentor is invaluable, and you should try to find one. Better yet, find multiple mentors. Good mentors can provide insight into your abilities and guidance toward your professional and personal development. Teachers, coaches, older siblings, and industry professionals can all qualify as mentors. They have personal and professional experience to share that will guide you to help make the right decisions for personal and professional development as well as reaching your goals.

▓ Benefits of Having a Mentor

While in high school and college I often felt lost. In my senior year in high school, I was very confused as I didn't know what I would be doing with myself after graduation. I didn't have any trade skills and my parents, having limited educational background, never discussed going to college as an option for me. When I finally decided to attend college a year and a half out of high school, it was a new experience that I had to figure out on my own. I listened to other students and followed them, sometimes with good results and other times not.

When I look back at it now, I can see I needed a mentor who had the experience of what I was going through to guide me through the proper steps of defining and reaching my goals. Instead of stressing and making wrong choices, mentors can help put you on the right path. Listed below are some of the benefits mentors provide to ease you through challenging times in your life.

- **Support** - After high school it can be intimidating to experience events for the first time as independent adults. It's an uncomfortable feeling that can result in loss of self-esteem and confidence. I know of people who lost confidence when they were young and dropped out of college after their first week. They were overwhelmed, uncomfortable, and not sure of themselves. Mentors are supportive in such situations. They understand what you are going through and can offer encouragement to help you gain the confidence you need to continue and move forward.

  Once, as a college professor, I reached out to a young individual who seemed overwhelmed. I wanted to make sure he didn't drop out, so I kept checking in with him. He asked me why I was helping him. I simply replied, "I was you once." That is the value of mentors. They experienced what you are experiencing at different times in your life so they can support you through some of your worst times.

  So, please, if at any time you are feeling overwhelmed and tempted to quit whatever it is you are doing, reach out to someone for support. Look to someone older in the family, older friends, or school counselors who have experienced what you are feeling. They can share their experiences and perform the actions of mentors by providing support and guiding you towards feeling more secure.

- **Define Goals** - Mentors can help you define objectives and goals. While you might know what your end goal is, for example, to graduate and get a job in your field of study, you will need to use a strategy to get there. Mentors can help you define objectives and smaller goals to help you reach your larger goals in the most strategically efficient ways possible.

    Mentors can help you choose the right classes as well as the teachers best for those classes. They can also provide advice on financing your education and resources you will need toward to graduation.

    For entrepreneurs, mentors can help you develop a plan to run your business and grow it in successful ways. They can help you define the resources you will need as well as strategies you need to follow for business success.

- **Accountable** - Mentors will check on you to help make sure you are on track to meeting your goals. You are responsible for fulfilling the requirements you discussed with your mentor. If there are any difficulties in achieving your objectives, you should discuss it with your mentor so that he/she can assist. Your mentor is doing his/her part and you will be expected do yours as well.

- **Learning** - Mentors will help you develop problem solving skills and discuss options towards reaching your goals. They are open to hearing your thoughts and will encourage you to come up with ideas. They are a wonderful resource to discuss the solutions you have come up with and will provide valuable feedback.

- **Good Habits** - Mentors will encourage you to form good habits and live your life with discipline. They will share what has worked for them and discourage activity that could be detrimental to your personal and professional goals. It's a very satisfying feeling to be on a strong and disciplined path toward your goals and experiencing all the successes that follow.

- **Social Network** - Mentors have several social connections they can reach out to for introductions to help you with development and career goals. They can connect you with people that provide internships and later in your career connect you to different people for professional employment opportunities.

    For entrepreneurs, networking is vital to creating a customer base. Mentors who are in business have established themselves in the community and beyond so that they can recommend you for jobs.

▓ **Multiple Mentors**

You can have multiple mentors at the same time as well as at different times in your life. For example, during high school, if you plan on going to college you will want to find someone who can guide you through the process of applying for college and sharing strategies to being accepted. Teachers can be very helpful in this area since they have had experience with it themselves and, most likely, mentored others through the process. But anybody who has had the experience, including fellow students, could be valuable in helping you through the process as well. I often like to listen to the advice of multiple people to learn different perspectives before coming to a conclusion.

If you plan on starting a business, you will want to find someone who can provide entrepreneurial experience to guide you accordingly. They can share their experiences to help you avoid the mistakes that so often occur for new business owners.

You may find your business has grown so big that you will need to find someone else who can provide suggestions and guidance on running a larger business. As you grow, so should your social capital for connecting with the right people to continue your journey.

As a college professor I have had the opportunity to mentor several students through their college years and beyond. You will find many teachers are willing to help in this way as well. You can ask them for assistance on choosing the right courses, deciding on a major, transferring to another college, and employment opportunities.

I helped one of the students I was mentoring at a community college choose the right courses and hired him as a student worker so that I could help him gain skills for employment. When it was time for him to transfer to a university, I connected him with a professor at the university who agreed to mentor him after me. So, as you grow your mentors should change accordingly.

Fellow students can also be mentors. As a student, I always took an interest in what other students were planning for their careers. It's a good way of not only learning what career opportunities are available, but what paths you should take to reach your goals.

I have always looked for someone with more life and work experience than me to learn from. I make it a point to listen to others with more experience to help guide me through my objectives. This includes college, employment, car purchases, home purchases, etc. People usually enjoy giving advice so don't be shy about asking.

Books

Books are very useful for mentoring because they provide unlimited opportunities to draw on the experiences of others. If you think about it, our perspectives are limited to our own experiences and interactions in life with people we meet. However, books provide an unlimited resource of experiences by people we will never meet. Reading can inspire and enhance our perspectives to help direct us on paths we may never have considered.

I am a firm believer that the more people we meet, the more we learn and the more our lives will be enhanced. Books provide the same opportunities without meeting anybody. You may even find that learning about the experiences of people through books provides more guidance in your life than the people you have met.

One of my favorite things to do is spend time at the Barnes and Noble Bookstore. While there, I pick up several books that interest me, find a seat, and read parts of each book. If I find I want to read any of the books in their entirety I purchase them.

Once I wanted to learn more about South African struggles, so I looked through several books and bought two, one on Steven Biko and the other on Nelson Mandela. I learned a great deal about South Africa through the eyes of these two strong leaders. I was inspired by their rationale and their commitment for the greater good. They taught me the importance of being dedicated to a cause and the virtue of patience and calmness even in the most challenging situations.

I enjoy reading biographies on various types of people such as world leaders, business leaders, and musicians because of how much they teach me about options in life. I especially enjoy reading about self-made people who started with struggling circumstances. Reading about such people provides learning experiences I wouldn't experience other-wise. Learning how others handled their struggles and used their motivation to succeed not only is inspirational, but it helps me plan for my own goals.

While in college, I read Benjamin Franklin's autobiography and became inspired by how he conducted his life. I learned he was the tenth child of seventeen children, grew up very poor, and had only two years of formal education beginning at eight and ending at ten. Yet, he persevered. Franklin educated himself by reading numerous books on his own, started a printing business, and became finan-cially successful enough to retire at the age of forty-two to dedicate the rest of his life to public service. He became a statesman and diplomat and is the only Founding Father to sign all documents leading to American independence, in-cluding the Declaration of Independence. It is amazing that a man born with so little had such an impact on America.

To get in the habit of reading you should read what interests you and not force yourself to read books because you are told they are good for you. Forced reading is forced learning and that is not the best way to learn. We learn best when we are truly interested. For example, although I was fond of Benjamin Franklin, you may not have any interest and that is okay. But find someone that you can learn from that does interest you instead.

Sometimes we start books and find as we get more into them, they are boring and we lose interest. That's okay and you shouldn't force yourself to get through it. Recently, I experienced reading an autobiography that started to bore me, so I skipped ahead to content more interesting. I still got something of the book, but I didn't force myself to read the whole book.

I have also stopped reading books altogether when I found them boring and moved on to other books. Don't let boring books deter you from reading. Keep looking for books that interest you and take that journey to learning.

▓ My Mentors

While I never had a true dedicated mentor, I understood later in life that there were people who were inspirational to me and that I learned from so, in fact, they were mentors. When I was a child, I watched my Uncle Jim. I looked at how he dressed, his impressive cars, how he presented himself, and how he talked to people he greeted them with a warm smile.

As I got older, I asked questions about his business. He owned a successful shoe repair shop and I saw his competitor down the street was charging less for new heels. I asked my uncle why customers would go to him if he was more expensive. His answer was, "Because I offer good service, I get things done with quality, and I get it done fast. I don't make the customers wait." I always remember this lesson in my life and apply it to my work and personal life. Any time I do something for someone, I do it with quality and speed.

While My Uncle Jim was very successful, a hard worker who drove fine cars and wore stylish clothes, what I most admired about him is how he loved people. He was always very caring and would go out of his way to please anybody in his presence. He especially loved children. For sure, he was my mentor and I picked up wonderful traits from him.

Then there's my Uncle Angelo. While he didn't know it, I was watching him too. He owned a tailor shop and I watched how he talked with his customers. It seemed like the customers enjoyed bringing their clothes there just so that they could converse with him. It seemed to me that connection with his customers was the soul of his business. It was obvious that he loved his customers, and they loved him.

Later in life I developed a strong relationship with my Uncle Angelo. I was very inquisitive about his path immigrating from Sicily with virtually no money and becoming a very successful businessman with his tailor shop as well as a successful musician. He was always a driven individual and interested in constantly educating himself. He at first played the drums in bands but later learned how to play the mandolin. Now he plays his mandolin and sings at various restaurants and music events, sometimes alone and other times with a whole band. While he sold his tailor shop, he continues to entertain with his music at the age of eighty-five. Anything is possible. So, even later in life, my Uncle Angelo inspires me.

🔳 Mentors We Never Met

While we may not interact with famous people, like books they can serve as mentoring opportunities indirectly. I like to find people who have been very successful and learn about their lives to find inspiration and direction from.

Recently, I was out with my family at a restaurant, and we had a nice young lady waiting on us who was enrolled in college. I always take interest in young people, so I asked her what her major was, and she said she was studying international law. I then asked if she knew who Amal Clooney is. She didn't so I suggested she look her up and read about her accomplishments for inspiration toward her own goals.

Amal Clooney is a Lebanese and British barrister (lawyer who specializes in representing clients in courts) who practices international law and fights for human rights. She has represented victims of genocide and sexual violence, and currently leads the legal task force on crimes committed in Ukraine.

Along with her husband, George Clooney, Amal founded the Clooney Foundation for Justice. In their own words:

"We founded the Clooney Foundation for Justice to hold perpetrators of mass atrocities accountable for their crimes, and to help victims in their fight for justice."

I find Amal Clooney to be an impressive, beautiful woman who is using her brilliance to help people in dire need. I think she is an excellent role model, and I would encourage anybody to learn about her impressive background.

Anybody that you look up to or learn from functions as a mentor even if they don't know it. Whether they are someone you met briefly and are not in regular contact with or a celebrity you never met, if you are inspired and learn from them, they can function as mentors for you.

I watch *Shark Tank* to learn about entrepreneurship as well as how the investors on the show strategize for successful investments. I also conduct further research on the show's investors to learn how they succeeded.

There are endless opportunities for you to seek mentorship, whether by direct contact, indirect contact, or reading. It's important that you learn from the experience of others. Many people have gone through the same circumstances in life that you are experiencing so take advantage of their experiences and learn the best way through the process.

I hope this chapter has shown you how valuable mentors are to assist in reaching your goals. Instead of having to learn everything through trial and error, mentors can share their experiences so that you can make the right choices toward a fulfilling life.

I also hope that you have been inspired to be a mentor yourself. Sharing your knowledge and experiences is wonderful gift to contribute to society.

Chapter 11

Balance and Strategy

"The key is not to prioritize what's on your schedule, but to schedule your priorities."

—STEPHEN COVEY

It is sometimes difficult to juggle so much that is happening in our lives. There is school, sports, work, family, social life, and many other commitments we need to juggle. But if you are to reach your goals and succeed, you will need to learn to be disciplined and prioritize your commitments.

Balancing Work and Studies

If you are in school, your schoolwork should be your number one priority. I say number one because along with your upbringing, it is the foundation of your life, both professional and personal. Education teaches us to manage our lives in society and is key to helping us make rational decisions as we go through life's challenges. The more you educate yourself, especially at a younger age, the easier and more successful your future will be.

You may need to work while going to school and that can have a take time away from your studies resulting negatively on your grade point average. Sometimes it's unavoidable as work is necessary to pay expenses. But there are ways to balance work and school to minimize the effect work will have on your study time.

While in college I had many expenses that I had to budget for, so I had to work. I had to pay for car expenses including a loan, insurance, and maintenance, help the family with household expenses, pay for my clothes, entertainment, and, of course, school, and associated expenses such as books. I worked at a grocery store weekdays starting at five p.m. and ending at ten p.m. On Saturdays, I worked eight hours starting at six a.m. and then Sunday for five hours starting at eight a.m.

My classes were scheduled Monday through Thursday starting at eight a.m. and ending mid-afternoon. In between classes I studied and then again a couple hours before work.

After work, I reached home around ten-thirty p.m. and did my best to stay awake with coffee so that I could study more. This, of course, is not the best way to go through college. My grades suffered greatly and the consequence of that was a low-grade point average that affected my ability to find good employment after college graduation.

In my last year of college, I came up with a strategy that helped me increase my grade point average by getting better grades with my remaining courses. I made the decision to cram all my courses into two days, Tuesdays and Thursdays. starting at eight a.m. and finishing around three p.m. I didn't have any breaks between classes to do any homework and I didn't attempt to do any before or after work. Instead, I rested before work at five p.m. and went to sleep after returning home at ten-thirty p.m.

The days I didn't have school, Monday, Wednesday, and Friday, I woke up early to start my studies promptly at seven a.m. My mind was fresh since I rested well, and I was able to spend the day studying without interruption from classes. With my mind rested and fresh, my ability to study and retain information improved greatly. The result was making the dean's list for the first time during my last two semesters in college. I wish I had thought of this strategy earlier. It would have made a big difference in my grade point average as well as my stress level.

While the above strategy worked for me, it may not work for you. I happen to do my best thinking in the morning and not so much in the afternoon, so it was perfect for me. Many others are different and are too groggy in the morning, so they may be more functional in the afternoon or evenings. You will have to understand how you best function and use that to your advantage to plan your schoolwork.

Most students I know had to work to go through college. If you do as well, try to manage your work hours so that they don't impede on your study time as well as the quality of your study time. You want to make sure your mind is at its best to process the material you are studying.

One idea for a job while in college is a front desk lobby security guard. Many professional buildings need night security guards at the entrance to help prevent any kind of criminal activity. This is a good opportunity to get paid while you are studying in peace since there is very little activity going on. Many of my college friends did this and I wish I had as well.

I also think it's a good idea to get a job as a student worker at the college you are attending. You will learn skills to help you with employment and your college employers will understand the importance of your studies. I once hired three student workers at the same time. I was concerned about their studies, so I let them know that was priority over the work they had to do for me. If they needed to take time off to study, I always granted it. Chances are other student managers will do the same.

◉ Balancing School Costs

One of the reasons I worked so much during college was because I wanted to minimize the amount of student loans I needed. I hated the thought of having large student loan debt after graduation, so I worked to keep my loans manageable and paid them off fairly quickly once I got a professional job. But there was a cost to that strategy, my grades and social life.

In hindsight, I see working so much harmed my grade point average and prevented me from joining many social activities that are so important for your development and social capital. If I worked less and applied for more student loans to support myself during college, my grades may have been better and I would have developed more social contacts, both of which are vital to employment and development.

I don't want you to think that I'm advocating for taking out more loans, working less, and making yourself more available for fun social activities. Instead, I am trying to demonstrate that you will need to balance things at school and in your life. Many times, what may be a good idea in the short term may not be the best for the long term.

I was very concerned about my student debt, so I worked many hours and sacrificed my grades. In the short term I achieved what I wanted, low student debt. But my lower grade point average would follow me in the long term. To start, I had difficulty in finding professional employment after college graduation. Then the type of jobs I was offered were second class compared to what the large corporations were offering. For example, many corporations have leadership programs for students right out of college leading to solid career paths within the company. I did not qualify because my grade point average wasn't high enough.

Also, later in life when I decided to enter graduate school, I learned that grade point averages play a role in admission to the programs. So be cognizant of both short term and long term goals. I think it's better to sacrifice in the short term for the longer term rewards.

If I had to do it over again, I would have put more focus on my grades and found employment where my studies took priority, like accepting a role as a front desk security guard as mentioned earlier. It's important to understand your options and balance them to make the right decisions for your future.

▩ Choosing a Car

If you can get by college without purchasing a car, I would advise you to do so because cars and their upkeep are quite expensive. In addition to the purchase of a car, there's insurance, maintenance, taxes, and gas you need to be concerned about. But if you are commuting to school and work, as I did, you may very well need a car so let's talk about strategies to car ownership.

There are various options you can take to purchasing a car and I will go through them for your consideration.

- **Cheap Used Car** - During college I bought used cars that were cheap enough so that I didn't require a loan. For me, this option proved to be the worst. Not only was it costly because of all the breakdowns, but it interfered with my studies too. I'll share one of the many breakdown stories with you.

    My college was around twenty miles away from where I lived and on a Friday night I was studying at the college until midnight because I had to get a lot of my assignments completed using their computers. In those days, we didn't have personal computers. The next day I had to be at work at seven a.m. I left the college, and it was pouring rain— horrible weather to drive in. While on the highway my car broke down. In those days we didn't have cell phones, so I had to wait for a police officer to come by. After about an hour, one did stop by and called a tow truck for me. After about another hour, the tow truck driver hooked up my car and offered me to ride with him to the garage he was towing my car to which was halfway to my home. Once I got to the garage, I had to hitchhike the rest of the way home, about seven miles, in the pouring rain. Someone picked me up and brought me within two miles of my house and I walked the rest of the way home. By then it was five a.m. so I showered and walked to work in the rain which was about a mile and a half away. I never got any sleep that night and while at work I pondered how I would come up with the money to get my car back.

I didn't have enough money to fix the car and the longer I left it at the garage the more costly it would be because I got charged storage fees each day the car was there. I borrowed the money from a good friend and was able to get my car back on the road and look forward to more breakdowns.

Breakdowns added stress to my life and took me away from my studies. It was a like a project to get my car on the road again. I always worried about when the car would be fixed and how to come up with the money to pay for it. It seemed never ending. To help budget for expected breakdowns, I put money aside so that I would be ready with cash when it happened.

I would not advise purchasing a cheap used car with high mileage, as I did. It ended up costing me more cash than taking a loan out, and worse, it took me away from my studies.

- **Reliable Used Car** - There are many reliable used cars you can consider. While I favor a couple makes and models, I don't feel comfortable advocating for them so I will leave it to you to do your research. You can easily search for "reliable used cars" on google and find all the information you need on the subject. Be aware of the mileage of used cars as reliability is dependent on it.

  Buying a reliable used car is a practical choice. Even better if you can afford to pay cash for it. If you need to take out a loan for a used car expect to pay more in interest than you would with a new car.

- **New Car** - This, of course, is one of the most reliable options, but also costliest. Once again, if you can afford to pay cash, it's an easy solution so there is nothing to talk about other than price negotiation which I will address later in this chapter. Taking out a loan for a new car will result in a sizable monthly payment. If you can handle that without sacrificing your grades because of work, then it's a good option for transportation. However, I know many students who worked excessive hours to make their monthly payments so think before you make this choice.

- **Leasing a New Car** - A lot of people frown on leasing cars because at the end of the term of the lease you don't own the car and you are limited to the number of miles you can drive the car. For example, if your car lease was contracted for 12,000 miles a year for a total of 36,000 miles after three years and you return the car with 40,000 miles, you will have to pay a cost for the additional miles above 36,000. In addition, if you return the car with any damage, you may have to pay for that as well. You can always purchase the car at the end of the lease and if you took care of it, it might make sense to do so if the price is right.

There was a time that I didn't think leasing a car was a good idea. But as I learned more about leasing, especially the ability to negotiate the lease as well as the purchase of the vehicle at the end of the lease, it made more financial sense in certain situations. For example, lease payments are considerably less than loan payments so to be able to focus on your grades and not worry about high monthly payments for transportation, it makes sense to get through your school years with a reliable car.

While purchasing a car with a loan might make better financial sense in the long term because you own the car when you pay off the loan, high monthly payments may result in more working hours that will interfere with your studies and your goal of graduating with a high grade point average. So, this is a good example that demonstrates setting up a short term goal for reliable affordable transportation while in school is a better option to serve your school goals as opposed to the long term goal of a car paid off.

Having had my bad experiences with used cheap cars, I was able to advise a young man attending college on his car purchases. He didn't have enough money saved to purchase a reliable used car, so I tried to convince him to lease a brand-new car instead. But he insisted, as I did when I was his age, that he didn't want monthly payments. So, he bought a ten-year-old car with cash and, well, it was cool looking too. His friends liked it.

Just like what I experienced buying cheap used cars, his car kept breaking down, costing him a lot of money and interfering with his studies. Like me, he had to arrange tow services and come up with the money to pay for the tows and the repairs. Often, it would take days for repairs, so he had to find alternate means of transportation including friends and Uber.

One day he called me saying he had enough and asked if I would help him with the lease of a car. I helped him negotiate a lease for $149 a month on a brand-new Honda Civic with $1,000 down. I even negotiated extending the annual mileage to 14,000 a year rather than the standard 12,000. That was back in 2016 so I don't know how close I could get to the same deal today, but it worked for him, and he was very happy with the decision. It ended up saving him money since he no longer had to pay for costly repairs and tow services on his other car. Now he had a new car under warranty, reducing his stress level and helping him focus more on his schoolwork.

While I have been successful at advising and guiding many young adults towards their goals, I've not been as successful convincing them to purchase a practical car to serve their best interest while in school. They instead purchase cars they find cool. I understand this as I was young once too and bought cars the same way. But keep in mind, once you have finished school and gained steady employment, the rewards of your hard work will follow, including the ability to purchase a car you desire.

🦡 Purchasing a Car

I teach Microsoft Excel and one of the projects I assign my students is an assignment showing different monthly payments dependent on interest rate and the price of the car. But before doing so I like to prepare them on what to expect when shopping for a car at a dealership because it can be very stressful and intimidating.

Quite often, the first question a car salesperson will ask is, "How much can you afford monthly?" You should avoid answering this question as the answer will allow them to change the price on the car to their favor. The spreadsheet below helps explain this. Let's say the dealership is prepared to sell the car for $20,000 at a two percent interest rate resulting in a payment of $350.56 a month. I have highlighted this in yellow. If you tell the salesperson you don't want to spend more than $400 a month the salesperson can increase the price of the vehicle as much as $2,500 in this example and still meet your monthly payment request highlighted in green.

Car Loan Payments						
Interest Rate	Price 1 20,000.00	Price 2 20,500.00	Price 3 21,000.00	Price 4 21,500.00	Price 5 22,000.00	Price 6 22,500.00
0%	$333.33	$341.67	$350.00	$358.33	$366.67	$375.00
0.50%	$337.59	$346.03	$354.47	$362.91	$371.35	$379.79
1%	$341.87	$350.42	$358.97	$367.52	$376.06	$384.61
1.50%	$346.20	$354.85	$363.51	$372.16	$380.82	$389.47
2%	$350.56	$359.32	$368.08	$376.85	$385.61	$394.37
2.50%	$354.95	$363.82	$372.69	$381.57	$390.44	$399.32
3%	$359.37	$368.36	$377.34	$386.33	$395.31	$404.30
3.50%	$363.83	$372.93	$382.03	$391.12	$400.22	$409.31
4%	$368.33	$377.54	$386.75	$395.96	$405.16	$414.37
4.50%	$372.86	$382.18	$391.50	$400.82	$410.15	$419.47
5%	$377.42	$386.86	$396.30	$405.73	$415.17	$424.60
5.50%	$382.02	$391.57	$401.12	$410.67	$420.23	$429.78
6%	$386.66	$396.32	$405.99	$415.66	$425.32	$434.99
6.50%	$391.32	$401.11	$410.89	$420.67	$430.46	$440.24
7%	$396.02	$405.92	$415.83	$425.73	$435.63	$445.53
7.50%	$400.76	$410.78	$420.80	$430.82	$440.83	$450.85
8%	$405.53	$415.67	$425.80	$435.94	$446.08	$456.22
8.50%	$410.33	$420.59	$430.85	$441.11	$451.36	$461.62
9%	$415.17	$425.55	$435.93	$446.30	$456.68	$467.06
9.50%	$420.04	$430.54	$441.04	$451.54	$462.04	$472.54
10%	$424.94	$435.56	$446.19	$456.81	$467.43	$478.06

To avoid this sales approach, you should purchase a car only when you are fully educated with the cost of the car, interest rates available to you, and the monthly payments. You don't need to have the salesperson calculate this out for you. Tell the salesperson you would rather hear the price of the car rather than discuss monthly payments. It is the price of the car you need to negotiate as you should have already determined your monthly payments on your own.

There are several payment calculators available on the internet to use so that you can figure out your monthly payments yourself. Here is a link to one that is simple to use.

https://www.bankrate.com/loans/simple-loan-payment-calculator/

As I said earlier, going to a car dealership and working with a salesperson can be very stressful and intimidating. I explain to my students that any time they feel uncomfortable there is nothing wrong with telling the salesperson the following line:

"I am not comfortable making a decision right now and I need some time to think this through and return on another day."

The salesperson may try to ask why you are feeling that way and try to keep you there to make his sale, but do not give in. You are the person who will be making a big decision so feel confident in needing to repeat yourself about feeling uncomfortable and returning another day. It's a polite but powerful way of removing yourself from a stressful situation.

≋ Complete Goals in a Timely Fashion

It's important to avoid procrastination and complete your goals in a timely fashion so that you can focus on other events that will come later in life. I know of people who are married with children and decide then to pursue their degrees. While it's never too late to go back to school, it's better if you can have time later in life to focus on important events such as family and not have to worry about homework and exams.

I like to tell students that if they are going to attend college they should complete their degree(s) in a timely manner so that they can move on to other goals. Too often young adults will skip semesters and return to college off and on. This will only prolong the goal and stay in their minds until they finally graduate.

Some people like to take a year off after high school before going to college and, while that is not what I would do, it's perfectly alright if that works best for you. But I hope if you choose this path that you pursue your degree shortly thereafter.

I went back to college at the age of forty-two for my master's degree and it put a great deal of stress on my marriage and me personally. For a year I did nothing with my wife and family. All I did was study and go to work. I'm glad I got my master's degree, but I sacrificed family for it. I wish I had completed my master's degree right after my bachelor's degree so that it didn't take me away from wonderful times with family that I can't get back.

I would like to suggest that you try to establish yourself by your late twenties if not sooner. This means being financially independent with your career established and in pursuit of larger goals including marriage and family. My wish is for you to be empowered and to become a contributing member of society sooner rather than later.

With proper goals and discipline, you will find that by embracing the challenges before you, you will reap the benefits that follow. Learn to prioritize all your responsibilities and understand the degree of commitment you will need to reach your goals. You have the power to reach any of your goals. So, go ahead and show the world what you can do.

Afterword

*"RIP to the opportunities we missed because
of shyness and low self-esteem."*
—Brad_onema

As a college professor I have had the wonderful opportunity to guide students towards developing self-esteem and confidence to reach any goals they chose. This book was written to reach a wider audience to do the same.

Too often young adults are left confused and indecisive on their path forward. Without proper support and guidance, opportunities will be missed resulting in long term struggles. It is my desire to help as many youths as possible to find security within themselves and to make the right choices that will serve them a lifetime.

May all that read this book find the self-esteem and confidence to live a fulfilling life full of successes and pleasures.

Best of travels to you.

Louis S. Sapia, Jr.

CPSIA information can be obtained
at www.ICGtesting.com
Printed in the USA
BVHW071259240323
661080BV00005B/277

9 781958 729380